1965

... DAYS

# voice and speech

# VOICE and SPEECH

## FOR EFFECTIVE COMMUNICATION

**HELEN GERTRUDE HICKS, M.A.**
*University of Virginia,*
*Northern Center*

formerly

*Associate Professor of*
*Speech and Dramatics,*
Hunter College of the
City of New York

**WM. C. BROWN COMPANY PUBLISHERS**
135 SOUTH LOCUST STREET    •    DUBUQUE, IOWA

Copyright © 1963
by
Helen Gertrude Hicks

Library of Congress Catalog Card Number:   63-11886

Manufactured by WM. C. BROWN CO. INC., Dubuque, Iowa
Printed in U. S. A.

## To Janet

for her unceasing encouragement, patience and invaluable editorial acumen, which focused like an X-ray eye on every page.

"For if the trumpet give an uncertain sound, who shall prepare himself for battle? So likewise ye, except ye utter by the tongue words easy to be understood, how shall it be known what is spoken? for ye shall speak into the air . . . . Therefore, if I know not the meaning of the voice, I shall be unto him that speaketh a barbarian, and he that speaketh shall be a barbarian

—I Corinthians XIV:8, 9, 11

# Acknowledgements

The author is grateful to her former students for the use of their interesting descriptions of voice and speech. She wishes to thank also Mr. Paul A. Napier of the Arlington Public Library, Arlington, Virginia, for his help in tracing many a literary description of voice and speech to its source. For these quotations, the author is particularly grateful and ... thank the many authors, agents and publishers who so generously permitted her to quote their books. She would thank, also, those authors and publishers for their permissions ... longer passages in the *Practice Reading Book* (Book III) where they are footnoted individually.

The author acknowledges, therefore, her debt and gratitude to the following:

BLACK, Publishers, London, for the quotation from *The Top of the Heap* by A. A. Fair (Earl Stanley Gardner).

CAMBRIDGE UNIVERSITY PRESS for the quotation from the introduction to Selec... *From the Poems* of Percy Bysshe Shelley.

THOMAS Y. CROWELL COMPANY for ... quotation from *Lincoln as Lawyer and Orator* by Joseph H. Choate.

DODD, MEAD & CO. for the lines from *Lepanto* from the *Collected Poems* of G. K. Chesterton.

DOUBLEDAY & COMPANY for the quotations from *Evensong* by Beverly Nichols, *Almayer's Folly* by Joseph Conrad, *Northwest Passage* by Kenneth Roberts, *Rain* and *The Razor's Edge* by Somerset Maugham, and *More Work for the Undertaker* by Margery Allingham.

FABER AND FABER, London, for the quotation from *Memoirs of a Fox-Hunting Man* by Siegried Sassoon.

FARRAR & RINEHART for the quotation from *The League of Frightened Men* by Rex Stout.

HAROLD OBER ASSOCIATES for the quotations from *A Pavilion of Women* by Pearl Buck.

HARPER & ROW for quotations from *Incredible Tales* by Gerald W. Johnson, *Peter Ibbetson* by Gerald Du Maurier, *The Web and the Rock* by Thomas Wolfe, *Point Counterpoint* and *Chrome Yellow* by Aldous Huxley.

HOUGHTON, MIFFLIN COMPANY for the quotation from *Raintree County* by Ross Lockridge.

ALFRED A. KNOPF, INC. for the quotations from *The Wall* by John Hersey, "*Obscure Destinies* by Willa Cather, and from *Mario and the Magician, Buddenbrooks,* and *The Magic Mountain* by Thomas Mann.

LITTLE, BROWN & CO. for the quotation from *The Last Hurrah* by Edwin O'Connor.

THE MACMILLAN COMPANY for the quotation from *Martin Eden* by Jack London.

JULLIAN MESSNER for the quotation from *Champion Road* by Frank Tisley.

F. MUELLER for the quotation from *The Homecoming* by Cecil Gordon Wimhurst.

NEW DIRECTIONS for the quotation from *A Child's Christmas in Wales* by Dylan Thomas.

W. W. NORTON & COMPANY for the quotation from *Mr. Gladstone* by W. P. Hall, and that from *Gielgud's Hamlet* by John Mason Brown in his collection of reviews, *Two on the Aisle,* (reprinted from the New York Post.)

OXFORD UNIVERSITY PRESS for the quotation from *John Gielgud's Hamlet* by Rosamund Gilder.

FREDERIK PROKOSCH for the quotations from his book, *Seven Who Fled.*

G. P. PUTNAM'S SONS for the quotation from *Ellen Terry and G. B. Shaw: A Corresdence* edited by Christopher St. John.

PYRAMID PRESS for the quotation from *The Gadfly* by E. K. Voynich.

RANDOM HOUSE for the quotation from *The Invisible Man* by Ralph Ellison.

CHARLES SCRIBNER'S SONS for the quotations from *Look Homeward Angel* and *Of Time and the River* by Thomas Wolfe.

NANCY DALLAM SINKLER for her "Postcript" in the Saturday Evening Post, March 3, 1951.

JAMES THURBER for permission to quote from his article, *Friends, Romans, Countrymen, Lend Me Your Earmuffs,* in THE NEW YORKER MAGAZINE of October 25, 1960.

THE VIKING PRESS for the quotations from *The Grapes of Wrath* by John Steinbeck.

A. WATKINS, Inc., author's agents, for the quotations from *Green Dolphin Street* by Elizabeth Goudge (copyright 1944 by the author) and from *Xingu* by Edith Wharton (copyright 1916 by Scribner's and 1944 by Elisina Tyler).

# Preface

In the strong conviction that the study of voice and speech for effective communication is not only worthwhile for the individual, but very much needed on a large scale, a series of three volumes for the earnest student's use is here offered. The *Text* is an exposition of the subject; the *Work Book*, assignments and exercises for developing the voice and sharpening the tools of articulation; and the *Reader*, which contains passing for refining vocal controls and articulation with the significance of expressiveness in communication.

The practical study of voice and speech is the use for effective use of a very important skill which everyone possesses to some degree of efficiency, involving muscular actions which are involuntary and habitual. The student must come to recognize these muscular actions as the physical realities of speech through a period of conscious awareness. In his study he must translate all information about the subject into performance and test the result in his ears. With the emphasis upon *doing*, therefore, the author has attempted to keep the textual exposition at a minimum, and to put it in such a way as to help the student create concrete mental images of sight and sound.

Furthermore, the student must acquire a clear awareness of what is desirable and what is undesirable in the actual sounds made by a speaker, to emulate the one and avoid the other. To this end a glossary of definitions and descriptions of both desirable and undesirable qualities is provided in parallel columns at the end of each chapter of the text. To this end, also, the first assignments in the *Work Book* are assignments in *listening*. The student is to listen to and describe, without criticizing, the voices and speech he hears about him. Without an ear trained for such discrimination there can be no successful voice training.

The complicated act of oral communication involves the smooth functioning of many physical parts in simultaneous performance, of which the first significant result of these interdependent actions is the production of voice. Since voice is the raw material that is moulded into speech, this author believes that speech training should begin with voice study. Then the development of a well controlled, flexible voice is carried on into the more sophisticated study of articulation.

Following this point of view the *Text* is divided into two parts: Part I: SOUND—the production of voice; and Part II—SOUND AND SENSE—the articulation of speech sounds into effective communication.

The *Work Book* follows the same order. In Part I for the development of voice the pages of assignments in listening are followed by exercises for the development of various qualities of and control over the voice. Use of these exercises should be followed by practice passages, the effective reading of which calls for particularly desirable voice qualities. In each practice session the student should proceed from exercises for sound alone to the expression of ideas. This is important to the realization that voice is not an end in itself, but an instrument of communication.

Part II of the *Work Book* follows the order of chapters in Part II of the *Text*. It contains assignments in word study and pronunciation in relation to each chapter as well as a continuation of the assignments in listening. The phonetic symbols of the International Phonetic Alphabet (IPA) are used extensively in Part II and the student should acquire a facility with them early in his study, for they are the only consistent device for writing the sounds of speech.

Throughout the *Work Book* blank pages are provided for the student to create exercises for himself, using the practice material of the *Work Book* as models. These blank pages could be, therefore, among the most important pages in the *Work Book*, for when the student creates his own practice material, he becomes an active seeker after his own improvement rather than a passive, however dutiful, pupil. As an active agent in his own behalf, he will make more rapid strides in his own progress.

The third volume of the series is a practice *Reading Book* which follows the same order as the other two. Here will be found passages, both short and long, for sustained and significant reading aloud, which, nevertheless, continue specific practice for the various vocal techniques, articulate correctness, and flexibility. This *Reading Book* begins where the *Work Book* leaves off and should be considered the climactic effort of the student's earnest and creative study. Its use provides both a motive for employing a particular vocal technique and the test of effectiveness of the speaker's communication. The selections for reading correspond to the songs a singer studies and prepares to sing. It is in the process of this preparation that the student increases the effective use of his vocal instrument and perfects his interpretative communication.

All three books could well be used concurrently. Along with the study of a chapter in the *Text* there should be immediate, correlative assignment in the *Work Book*. This should be followed by assignment of passages in the *Reading Book* selected for practice of the same vocal techniques and speech sounds being concurrently studied in the *Text* and worked on in a corresponding section of the *Work Book*.

Whether or not the instructor wishes to amplify the text or the practice material, the book is intended to provide a framework upon which the student may build a course of study and practice for himself which can go on far beyond the time limits of the course. The student must realize always, however, that the goal of his efforts should be to develop his speaking voice, not for the sake of acquiring a "pear-shaped tone" but to develop an instrument of effective communication.

This text and its accompanying practice books are the product literally of thousands of Hunter College of the City of New York for the past thirty years, as well as my many friends and colleagues across the country, have contributed to it directly or indirectly. The author is grateful for their many contributions to the book and to the honing of her own tools of teaching speech through the years. She is happy to acknowledge special indebtedness to Dr. Ota Thomas Reynolds, Chairman of the Department of Speech and Dramatics, and to Dr. Helen Downey, Associate Professor of Physiology, both of Hunter College of the City of New York; to Mrs. Zelda Horner Kosh, Vice President of Greater Washington Educational Television Association, Director of Program Development of WETA, Washington, D.C.; and to Dr. Thomas Lewis, Professor of Speech and Dean of the Graduate School, Florida State University. Finally, the author is indebted to her sisters, Mrs. Dorothy Hicks McColl, teacher of music in the Public Schools of Adrian, Michigan, and Mrs. Marjory Hicks Benedict of the National Science Foundation, Washington, D.C., for their continuous prodding and critical interest. All these friends and colleagues have given generously of their time and thought in reading parts of the manuscript, and their considered suggestions have been put to use for the betterment of the book.

Helen Gertrude Hicks

# Illustrations

# Table of Contents

## PART I — SOUND

## PART II — SOUND AND SENSE

# voice and speech

# PART I - SOUND

## The Production of Voice

✿　　✿　　✿

O what is it that makes me tremble so at voices?
Surely whoever speaks to me in the right voice, him or her
　　I shall follow,
As the water follows the moon, silently with fluid steps,
　　anywhere around the globe.
All waits for the right voices;
Where is the practiced and perfect organ? Where is the
　　developed soul?
For I see every word uttered thence has deeper, sweeter,
　　new sounds, impossible on less terms.

I see brains and lips closed, tympans and temples unstruck,
Until that comes which has the quality to strike and to
　　unclose,
Until that comes which has the quality to bring forth what
　　is slumbering forever ready in all words.

　　　　from LEAVES OF GRASS by Walt Whitman

# Chapter I

# The Human Instrument

The most sensitive and flexible musical instrument is the human voice. Every human being is born with an instrument capable of producing a great number of sounds. Some of these human sounds have been produced over and over again, more or less uniformly, and so codified into language; some of them are shades and subtleties of tones, which move up and down by steps and glides of the voice in varied patterns of melody. The sounds are the recognized vowels and consonants of any language, and by their combinations the intellectual content of ideas is communicated, while the variations of voice convey the emotional significance and establish the full meaning.

Each human being learns to "play" his instrument to some degree of intelligibility by imitation of those around him. But, as with every acquired skill, a fine proficiency of voice and speech production is attainable only through deliberate training to perfect the smooth operation of all the actions involved. The object of voice training should be to bring all the mechanical pieces of apparatus into well controlled, coordinated operation instantly responsive to the stimulus of the ideas to be expressed.

## SOUND IS GENERATED

The instrument itself is a very small mechanism: two thin bands, THE VOCAL BANDS, or vocal cords. They lie at the top of the TRACHEA (the windpipe) in the path of the outgoing breath stream. The space between the vocal bands is known as the GLOTTIS. Such a delicate instrument as these vocal bands must be protected, hence the cartilaginous structure of the LARYNX (the voice box) surrounding it. The impulse to speak is a nerve impulse which brings the vocal bands together, narrowing the glottis to a tiny slit. The out-going breath stream passes through the glottis, sets the bands in vibration, producing sound.

The generation of sound, or PHONATION, is similar to the generation of sound in the oboe of an orchestra in that air is expelled between thin reeds which vibrate, setting up waves of sound. But, unlike the reeds of the oboe, the human vocal bands change in length, thickness and tenseness *during the production of sound*, with corresponding variations in pitch levels. In this respect the human instrument may be compared to the stringed instruments of the orchestra in that the player changes the length of the vibrating string to change pitch as he continues to play, and the sound generated by the vibrating strings moves from note to note. Or, perhaps, an even more apt and simple comparison would be that of a stretched rubber band which may be pulled more, or less, taut while vibrating, thus creating waves of sound which vary in pitch with the tautness or looseness of the bands. PHONATION and PITCH will be dealt with further in Chapter 3.

## SOUND IS AMPLIFIED

The sound waves generated in the larynx, however, cannot be heard unless they are amplified many times. The breath stream, now carrying sound waves, proceeds on its way out of the body. First it enters the PHARYNX, commonly called the throat, which offers the first amplification. The pharynx is a chamber located above the larynx at the back of the mouth and behind the uvula, an extension of the soft palate which you can see hanging downward toward the back of the tongue. From the throat the vocalized breath stream moves forward through the resonating ORAL CHAMBER under the "sounding board" of the PALATE and thence out into space. Sympathetic vibrations set up in the SINUSES and NASAL PASSAGES amplify the higher keys, while the lower keys are amplified in the great cavity of the THORAX (the chest). Thus, amplifing the human voice is much like sending sound waves through a French horn in the orchestra. The generated sound wave proceeds through the convolutions of the horn, setting up sympathetic vibrations in its hollow chambers, reinforcing the original sound. The amplification of voice is the problem of RESONANCE and will be dealt with further in Chapter 4.

## SOUND IS PARTICULARIZED

Finally, the vocal instrument is capable of a feat unique to itself. The oral chamber may assume a number of shapes and sizes while the voice is flowing through it. These changing shapes of the oral chamber create a great many distinctly different sounds known as VOWELS and CON-SONANTS. Putting vowels and consonants together into syllables of sound and the syllables into words is articulation, which will be studied in detail in Part II: SOUND AND SENSE. Effective oral communication depends upon distinction and accuracy of articulation by the speaker for quick logical comprehension by the listener, but for full significance of meaning words must be spoken with correspondingly correct and expressive qualities of voice.

## TO SUMMARIZE

The human instrument is like the reed instruments of an orchestra in generation of sound (PHONATION), like the stringed instruments in its changes of PITCH, like the horns in the amplification of sound (RESO-NANCE) to make it audible, and like no other instrument in its ability to produce an infinite variety of sounds (ARTICULATION). Since all these actions must take place simultaneously, a finely co-ordinated p........................ ... .. .... ...... .......ed must be perfected in order to gain ease and proficiency in playing the human instrument which is the human voice.

\* \* \*

### THE QUALITY OF IT

"Never, in all the women he had heard speak, had he heard a voice like hers. . . . It was the quality of it, the repose, and the musical mod-ulation—the soft, thick, indefinable product of culture and a gentle soul. As he listened to her, there rang in the ears of his memory the harsh cries of barbarian women and of hags, and, in lesser degrees of harshness, the strident voices of working women and of girls of his own class."

—in MARTIN EDEN by Jack London.

# GLOSSARY

## VOCAL QUALITIES

### DESIRABLE

1. *A CLEAR VOICE.* A voice of focused purity of tone, unforced, of fine timbre.

   "She had a clear, crisp voice which was enchanting to listen to. It made one think of the Fall when the wind rustles through the leaves and there is a bit of music as it passes."
   —by a student

### UNDESIRABLE

1. *UNCLEAR.* A wheezy, husky, breathy voice; a hoarse, throaty, hard voice; a heavy, rumbling voice.

   "He had a very deep voice, indistinct, and without, so to speak, a clearly defined contour. 'A furry voice,' his daughter Lucy called it when she was a child."
   —POINT COUNTERPOINT
       by Aldous Huxley

2. *A FLEXIBLE VOICE.* A voice capable of smooth changes in volume, pitch, tone.

   "Montanelli's voice was rather low, but full and resonant, with a silver purity of tone that gave to his speech a peculiar charm. It was the voice of a born orator, rich in possible modulations. When he spoke to Arth, its note was always that of a caress."
   —in THE GADFLY
       by E. K. Voynich

2. *TIGHT, PINCHED.* A choked, pinched quality, often shrill, tight, whining.

   "Her voice was like that of a cricket in the bushes, lamenting shrilly the approach of winter."
   —of Mlle. Michonneau in
   PERE GORIOT
       by Honoré Balzac

3. *A WARM VOICE.* A voice that is vibrant and sympathetic, in a medium low key, with just the right amount of resonance.

   "If human voice could be transposed into color, hers would be only a soft lavender hue, so warm and delicate, so rich and enveloping were its tones."
   —by a student

3. *COLD, SHARP, HIGH.* A hard, flat, steely quality, usually striking a high key; narrow in range.

   "The most remarkable thing about her was her voice, high, metallic, and without inflection; it fell on the ear like the pitiless clamor of the pneumatic drill."
   —of Mrs. Davis in RAIN
       by Somerset Maugham

"His voice was like cold lino-
leum on bare feet."
—of John Garner Billings, III
in TOP O' THE HEAP
by A. A. Fair

4. *A VOICE EASILY HEARD.* A
voice of adequate strength,
easily adjustable to the demands
of the physical surroundings and
the occasion.

"Her slightly veiled v o i c e
reached the listeners in the
theatre without any apparent
effort, though the nervous ath-
leticism behind it was of champ-
ionship quality."
—of Ellen Terry, described
by G. B. Shaw in Preface
CORRESPONDENCE
edited by C. St. John

4a. *WEAK, FAINT.* A voice that
has so little tone or force in it
that it seems far, far away; "a
monstrous little voice."

"His voice was like a strand of
silk being slowly and rhythmi-
cally unravelled from the silken
mask which hid him."
—of an Old Oriental in
SEVEN WHO FLED
by Frederik Prokosch

"Her voice was very light, coming out like whiffs of beaten
—by a student

4b. *LOUD, BOOMING.* A voice
that has too much volume and
force, that booms out with over-
whelming energy and with no
modulation.

"Her voice!—like the passing of
a train through a tunnel: booming, thundering, enveloping."
—by a student

"Instantly I was reminded of a
hot jazz band with a screeching
brass section. He spoke in a
loud, coarse voice, noisily sounding off for the sake of attention."
—by a student

*   *   *

"His voice came rushing at me in torrents. Its full, deep, sonorous tones
possessed many of the qualities of an electric storm in all its splendor.
Yet the warmth and color of his speech brought to mind the rainbow
which follows the storm."

—by a student

# Chapter II

## Breathing

The voice that reaches the ear of a listener is the result of three large and complicated mechanical and physical actions within the body. Each of these actions involves the smooth operation of many muscles, some working simultaneously, some in succession, a chain of cause and effect. A look at the various pieces of apparatus, in order to make a sharp mental photograph, as it were, should be helpful. A brief explanation of the working of all parts should turn that photograph into a mental moving picture of the three successive actions which produce the voice: BREATHING, PHONATION, RESONANCE.

### BREATHING MUSCLES MOVE DOWN AND UP; OUT AND IN

The amount and force of air in producing voice are determined by the actions of three large sets of muscles, the INTERCOSTAL MUSCLES, the ABDOMINAL MUSCLES, and the DIAPHRAGM. The action of the diaphragm is basic to the action of the other two. Actually the diaphragm is a whole sheaf of muscles welded together into a dome of muscle which separates the THORAX (chest cavity), housing the respiratory system, from the ABDOMEN, housing the digestive system. It is at once the floor of the thorax and the ceiling of the abdomen. (Figure 1)

If we visualize the abdomen as a huge, inflated balloon, the diaphragm is then the top of the inflated balloon. Now, if the top of the balloon were pushed down, the balloon would expand just below the flattened top to compensate for the pressure from above. This compensating expansion movement is simultaneous with and equal to the movement downward of the top of the balloon. Thus, in the body as the diaphragm moves down and up in response to the rhythmic impulses of the nerve gov-

8

erning it, there is simultaneously a noticeable movement of the upper abdominal muscles out and in *which can be seen and felt.* At the same

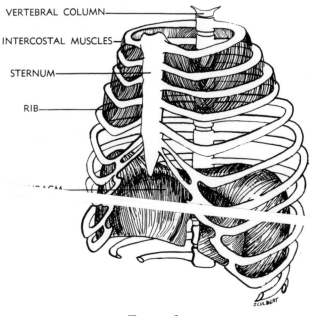

VERTEBRAL COLUMN

INTERCOSTAL MUSCLES

STERNUM

RIB

FIGURE 1

THORAX AND DIAPHRAGM SHOWING THE RIB CAGE AND INTERCOSTAL MUSCLES.

time there is an expansion of the lower chest walls made __ __ of the lower ribs and the intercostal muscles. Expansion takes place, then, just above the waistline with little perceptible movement in the upper chest. The actions of the alternate contraction and relaxation of the diaphragm, and the simultaneous expansion and retraction of the upper abdominal wall and the lower chest wall take place outside the thorax. Now let us see what happens within the thorax in direct response to these outer actions.

## THE LUNGS ARE INFLATED AND DEFLATED

The cause and effect relationship of the diaphragm and the LUNGS may be readily understood by studying the Hering apparatus (Figure 2).

The glass jar with its rubber bottom and corked neck is airtight, in the same manner as the thorax is airtight; the Y-tube and the balloons attached act in precisely the same way as the TRACHEA and the LUNGS.

A                                                   B

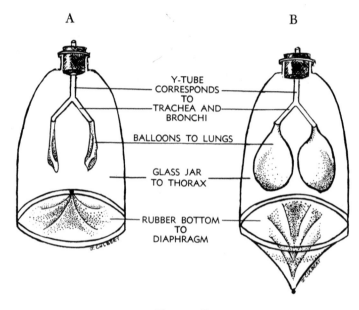

Y-TUBE
CORRESPONDS
TO
TRACHEA AND
BRONCHI

BALLOONS TO LUNGS

GLASS JAR
TO THORAX

RUBBER BOTTOM
TO
DIAPHRAGM

FIGURE 2
HERING'S APPARATUS.
Hering's apparatus, corresponding to the thorax with diaphragm, lungs and trachea, demonstrates the performance of exhalation and inhalation within the thorax.

In the thorax the walls are extensible, whereas in the Hering jars they are rigid. Now let us take note of the finely coordinated interaction of all these parts. When the elastic, rubber bottom of the jar is pulled down, the cubic content of the jar is enlarged. The resulting decrease of air pressure within the jar inflates the balloons and air flows in from the outside, from greater pressure to lesser pressure,* down the Y-tube and into the inflated balloons. Let the elastic bottom go back to the position of A of Figure 2. Now the capacity is decreased, the pressure

*Boyle's Law. When a gas is subjected to compression and kept at a constant temperature, the product of the pressure and volume is a constant quantity; that is, the volume is inversely proportioned to the pressure.

increased, and action within the jar is reversed. The air in the balloons moves up the Y-tube and out, flowing again from greater to lesser pressure, but this time in the opposite direction, and the balloons collapse. It should be noted here that the *rate* of intake and expulsion of air is in exact relation to the *rate* of movement of the elastic bottom down and up. Movement of air in and out, therefore, is controlled by the movement of the elastic bottom of the jar.

Substitute the thorax for the glass jar, the diaphragm for the rubber bottom, the lungs for the balloons, the trachea and bronchi for the Y-tube, and you can visualize the action of inhalation and exhalation within the human chest. But, as we have seen, this action is as dependent upon the action of the upper abdominal and intercostal muscles as upon the diaphragm. It is the action of these outer muscles that can be seen and felt and so *can be consciously controlled*. Now let us study the two figures below (Figure 3) showing expansion of the upper abdomen and thorax during inhalation and contraction during exhalation.

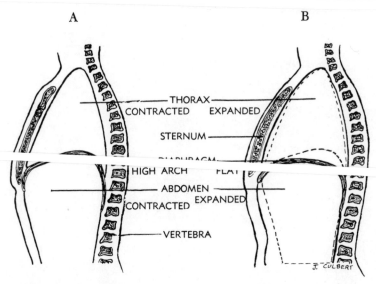

A

B

THORAX
CONTRACTED    EXPANDED

STERNUM

DIAPHRAGM
HIGH ARCH    FLAT

ABDOMEN
CONTRACTED    EXPANDED

VERTEBRA

J. CULBERT

A. EXHALATION
Contraction of thorax and abdomen with arched diaphragm.

B. INHALATION
Expansion of thorax and abdomen with flattening of diaphragm.

FIGURE 3
BODY MOVEMENTS DURING RESPIRATION.

To complete our set of pictures of the performance of breathing we should include the passive organs of breathing, those which are acted upon and have no power in themselves. Below is a sketch of the lungs, the trachea and bronchi, with the larynx as an extension of the trachea (Figure 4).

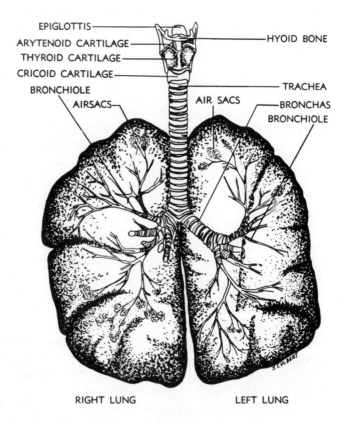

EPIGLOTTIS
ARYTENOID CARTILAGE
THYROID CARTILAGE
CRICOID CARTILAGE
BRONCHIOLE
AIRSACS
AIR SACS
HYOID BONE
TRACHEA
BRONCHAS
BRONCHIOLE
RIGHT LUNG          LEFT LUNG

FIGURE 4

LUNGS, BRONCHI, TRACHEA AND LARYNX, PASSIVE ORGANS OF BREATHING.

The trachea and lungs are merely passageway and reservoir respectively for the air that streams in and out during "Operation Breathing."

## TO SUMMARIZE

The mechanics of breathing are, briefly, as follows. The diaphragm, which is both the floor of the thorax and the ceiling of the abdomen, moves down. The resulting displacement of air below pushes out, or expands, the muscles below the waistline (the abdominal wall). At the same time the downward movement of the diaphragm (as the floor of the chest) decreases the air pressure within the thorax, expanding the lungs. Moving from greater to lesser pressure, air flows into the body from the outside through the nose or mouth, down the trachea and into the expanded lungs. This is INHALATION. It is important to note that the *amount of air intake* is determined by the *amount of movement* of the large muscles in the region of the waistline and can be voluntarily controlled.

As soon as sufficient air is taken into the lungs (the amount varies according to the need, physical activity, etc.), the actions of the dia- phragm and the other breathing muscles are reversed. Slowly the walls recede, the floor rises, the lungs _____ the air moves up the trachea and out, *in exact response to the timing and force of the breath- ing muscles* dictated by the force and amount of breath *needed to speak* or to perform any other physical feat. This is EXHALATION.

For the study of voice it is more important to control the manner and the amount of exhalation than of inhalation for it is the outgoing breath stream that generates sound as it plays upon the vocal bands. The amount of exhaled breath, the rate of exhalation, the evenness of the flow of the outgoing breath stream, even the direction of it through the mouth or _____ the nose affects the quality of the voice. We have seen how the flow of air into and out of the lungs is regulated directly by the ac- tion of the breathing muscles. It would seem obvious, then, that control over the action of these muscles is control over the outgoing breath stream and, consequently, control over voice production. To develop strong muscles of breathing and to establish a smoothly rhythmic, co- ordinated action of all the breathing muscles practice Exercise I in the *Work Book* as basic to all other exercises.

❂   ❂   ❂

"The voice babbled on like a stream of air slowly escaping from a leaky balloon, until, with a faint hiss, it collapsed."

—by a student

# GLOSSARY

## TECHNIQUES OF BREATHING

### DESIRABLE

1. *THORACIC-ABDOMINAL BREATHING.* A technique of breathing for power, endurance and control in any physical activity. A noticeable expansion takes place in the lower chest and upper abdomen, above and below the waistline, allowing full inhalation and smooth, controlled exhalation on which the voice rides evenly and clearly with controlled power.

"William Jennings Bryan could speak to thirty thousand people in the open air and make every word heard at the fringes of the crowd without the aid of microphones and amplifiers or any other mechanical device. . . . At his most impassioned he seemed to be well within his limits, with plenty of reserve power still untouched, and this gave an extraordinary effect of mastery to his utterance."

—in INCREDIBLE TALES
by Gerald W. Johnson

### UNDESIRABLE

1. *CLAVICULAR-UPPER CHEST BREATHING.* Shallow breathing with little power, endurance or control. The shoulders are raised, the upper chest expands, the waistline is pulled in against the diaphragm, preventing full movement, full inhalation. Exhalation rushes forth uncontrolled. There is a burst of voice at the beginning of a word group, little at the end, necessitating short, quick gasps of breath between words in awkward, short, audible intervals.

"Taking gasps of breath after every three or four words, she sounded as though she had just run a race."

—by a student

# Chapter III

---

## Phonation and Pitch

---

The second step in voice production is the generation of sound, or PHONATION, by using the exhaled breath stream to vibrate the vocal bands. In Figure 4 (p. 12 of Chapter 2) you must have noted the curious cup-like enlargement at the top of the trachea. This is the larynx, a cartilaginous structure which houses the sensitive and delicate vocal bands, part of the musical instrument of the human voice. Their primary function is to generate sound waves.

## THE VOCAL BANDS ARE PLAYED UPON BY THE BREATH

As you are silently reading this, the vocal bands within your larynx are completely relaxed and wide apart, as in Figure 5, below. They are joined together at one end and form an apex; at the other end they are attached to two pieces of cartilage which on the impulse to speak pivot

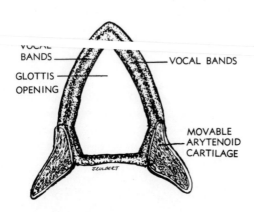

VOCAL BANDS

GLOTTIS OPENING

VOCAL BANDS

MOVABLE ARYTENOID CARTILAGE

FIGURE 5
POSITION OF VOCAL BANDS DURING SILENCE.

and pull the two elastic vocal bands practically together, closing the space between the bands to a tiny slit. During silent breathing, however, there is a large triangle of space between the bands known as the glottis. Quite obviously, air can pass through the wide open glottis with the greatest of ease without disturbing the vocal bands. The impulse to speak, a brain-nerve impulse to the movable cartilage, brings the two vocal bands into parallel position (Figure 6) with the glottis a mere slit between them. Now a stream of air passing through the glottis between the vocal bands will set them in vibration, and generate waves of sound. This is PHONATION, the second step in voice production. Breath, then, is the generator of the human voice, the power and the motor. It should play on

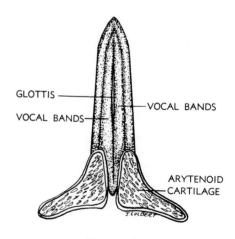

FIGURE 6
VOCAL BANDS IN POSITION FOR SPEECH.

the vocal bands with a technique of gentle firmness to insure good phonation. Obviously, techniques of breath control must be acquired. A discussion of breath control in relation to all phases of voice production will be found in Chapter 5, climaxing and summarizing Part I—SOUND—as produced by the musical instrument of the human voice.

## CHANGE TENSION; CHANGE PITCH

In the continuous passage of breath through the closed glottis vocal sounds may be produced in a variety of pitch or keys. In position for voice production the bands are capable of change within themselves while they are actually vibrating. Much as an elastic band will give out a higher pitch while vibrating if it is stretched tighter and thinner, so the vocal bands vibrate with varying pitch changes, higher or lower, as the bands themselves tighten or release tensions, become thinner or thicker, longer or shorter. Thus, in this second step of voice production—phonation—we not only originate vocal sound, but vocal sounds of varying pitch, and can do so both involuntarily and voluntarily.

From observation of stringed instruments we note that the higher the pitch, the faster the vibration of the string, the shorter its movement through space, and the shorter its wave length; the lower the pitch, the slower the vibration of the string, the longer its movement through space, and the longer its wave length. So, too, with the human instrument which gives to every human being a voice with a wide range of pitch from high to low, from low to high. A very important factor in effective speaking and expressiveness is the use of a variety of pitch levels of the voice.

## TO SUMMARIZE

Again it is muscle action that makes sound possible by bringing the vocal bands into position to be played upon by the expiring breath. Again the muscles must act with flexible ease, as well as with firm strength. The vocal bands must not be brought too tightly together, closing the glottis completely, for the forcing of the stream of air between the tightly closed bands will create an explosiveness, especially of syllables beginning with vowels, and the voice will be unpleasantly hard. On the other hand, if the bands are too loose and flabby and the space between them too great, there will be a fuzzy breathiness in the voice and a colorless monotony in the pitch.

* * *

"Her voice sounded like a hoarse snicker, a strange, high, husky and derisive falsetto, which seemed to prod him in the ribs."
—in OF TIME AND THE RIVER by Thomas Wolfe

# GLOSSARY

## PHONATION

### DESIRABLE

1. *"FREE AND EASY."* The voice begins to flow easily and without apparent effort. The vocal bands are close together, but not too tightly, nor too loosely so. The force of the breath is light but firm.

. . . "Her voice was ever soft, Gentle and low—an excellent thing in woman."
—of Cordelia in KING LEAR, V:3
                by Shakespeare

"Her voice was like sunshine on growing corn, a clear blue sky, or birds singing; fresh, clean and alive."

                —by a student

### UNDESIRABLE

1. *FORCED, HARSH, METALLIC.* The voice seems to burst from the speaker in loud, grating tones. The bands are too tight and tense, too close together, even overlapping; the muscles around them are too tightly constricted. The force of the breath is heavy and uncontrolled, coming with a rush, like an avalanche of water through a sudden break in a dam.

"The one blemish was the shrill, harsh, discordant voice . . . which was chiefly observable when he spoke under excitement. Then his voice was not only dissonant, like jarring strings, but he spoke in sharp fourths, the most unpleasant sequence of sound that can fall upon the human ear."

—of Percy Bysshe Shelley, in INTRODUCTION TO SELECTIONS FROM THE POEMS OF SHELLEY
                —Cambridge Edition

2. *LEGATO CLARITY.* The voice flows in a smooth line of sound from syllable to syllable. The force of the breath behind it is even and easy; the muscles holding the vocal bands in close proximity are firm, but not too tight, in quiet, even tension, never fluttering unevenly, closing the glottis tightly, nor opening it suddenly.
"Lynn Fontanne's cadences you can't forget, the way her voice

2. *GLOTTALIZATION.* The voice seems to stop as if it were swallowed suddenly, and start again with some violence, giving a hard edge to initial vowels, almost as if they were being "kicked" out. Consonants in the middle of words—the *t* in *bottle*, in *shuttle*—seem to be gulped down. The glottis has been closed tightly, cutting off the flow of voice suddenly; then the breath forces the bands

touches the words and smoothes them out."

—in THE SECRET PATTERN
by Celia Cole

"Oh, when she speaks, to all
her words give ear,
Feeling how soft, how gracious
is their flow,
That doth the ear with choicest
phrase beguile."
—of Beatrice in
THE PORTRAIT
by Dante

apart in a succession of harsh attacks.

"She spat out her words as if they were machine gun bullets mowing down an enemy."
—in CHAMPION ROAD
by Frank Tisley

"It was an intense, emphatic voice, and the words came out in g u s h e s, explosively, as though they were being forced through a narrow aperture under emotional pressure."
—in POINT COUNTERPOINT
by Aldous Huxley

3. *FOCUSED CLARITY.* T h e ~~voice is the~~ out-going breath stream that is allowed to pass through the glottis is vocalized during phonation. There is no escaping breath surrounding the voice.

"The traveler had been chained to the spot . . . by the charm of Dinah's mellow treble tones. The simple things she said seemed like novelties, as a mel- ~~ody strikes us~~ with a new feeling when we hear it sung by the pure voice of a boyish chorister . . ."

—in ADAM BEDE
by George Eliot

"His voice is as rich and smooth as fine-textured, claret-colored velvet."

—by a student

3. *FUZZY, HUSKY, RASPY.* A ~~huskiness, hoarseness, a "fuzzi-~~ ness on the edges, a breathiness surrounds the tone, spreading it out of focus, as it were. The vocal bands are flabby and too loosely drawn together, or are prevented from coming together by nodules on the vocal bands; or tight constriction of the throat muscles, forcing the bands to rub together as they vibrate, has caused them to become inflamed and roughened, and to develop ~~little~~ "corns" on the bands.

"Like a crust of dry bread being grated, her voice rasped on our ears with a steady monotone. It wore itself out by the end of a sentence, leaving nothing but a welcome silence."

—by a student

"Her voice was bog-husky, sounding as though strained through some rough material."
—by Truman Capote

PITCH

1. *WIDE RANGE.* A voice that strikes a wide range of keys from high to low in a lively and interesting pattern of speech; a melodious voice. The vocal bands, strong and flexible, easily change in tension, length and thickness, creating a variety of keys in response to the need for emphasis and variety of expression.

"It was a pleasure to hear Larry talk, because he had a wonderfully melodious voice; it was light, rich without being deep, and with a singular variety of tone. It was very persuasive. It was like balm."

—of Laurence Darrell in
THE RAZOR'S EDGE
    by Somerset Maugham

1. *NARROW RANGE.* A voice that moves within a compass of no more than three notes of the scale, sliding up and down in intervals of half and even quarter tones, creating an effect of monotone and showing no interest or aliveness in response to idea and emotion. The whole vocal apparatus is too relaxed, with little or no power; performs perfunctorily and lazily.

"This teacher's voice was like the dull, thudding beat of rain upon a roof on a chill winter night. At first you listen, but then, because there is no change of pitch or pace, you sink down in your coat collar as you sink into your warm bed on a rainy night."

—by a student

2. *MATURE, MEDIUM LOW KEY.* The most desirable pitch, ranging from middle *C* to *G* or *A*, or even upper *C*, with occasional excursions above and below for variety and emphasis. The vocal bands vibrate healthily along a five to eight-note reach with easy flexibility.

"Her voice, well-modulated and very pleasant, sounded happy and, like her face, seemed to have a rosy glow about it."

—by a student

"Her voice, cool and clear, measured, yet full, traversed as wide a range as possible for the human voice, but was of medium pitch generally, suitable for a woman of her stature and poise.

2a. *IMMATURE, HIGH PITCHED.* The pitch is constantly high and generally confined to a limited range of not more than three notes from *A* above middle *C* to upper *C*. The effect is very childish. Doubtless from habit, the voice has continued its childhood pattern of high, often whining, treble. Such immaturity is often the result of psychological causes, such as continued, excessive dependence on parental security.

"Her pitch was high and she spoke rapidly. It sounded as though someone had put a phonograph record on at the wrong speed."

—by a student

Its variability of force and range made the listener realize the heights and depths of emotions that might be revealed by human expression through the voice alone."

—by a student

"He had a high, sonorous, countrified voice which often trailed off in a comical drawl."

—of Mr. Leonard in
LOOK HOMEWARD, ANGEL
by Thomas Wolfe

2b. *TOO LOW PITCH.* A voice that stays too long in the very low keys, seeming to come from "way down under," moving through a very narrow range below middle *C* and rarely emerging from the depths. At first, very rich and unctuous sounding on the ears, a soft caress, it soon loses the definite contour and character of speech, and the mind of the listener drifts away.

"His voice could be comp̲ to a piece of delicious pastry— rich, thick, heavy. At first we find it delightful, but after too much repetition it becomes indigestible."

—by a student

"His voice was full and low, as if its battery were running down."

THE ABSENT-MINDED MURDERER
by Cornell Woolrich

❀          ❀          ❀

"Miss E's voice was that of a tragedian, low in key and monotonous in pace. Her friend's was the opposite; generally high-pitched, it travelled up and down the scale of her range, like a glissando in music."

—by a student

"Mrs. Ryder's voice was a thin factory-whistle wail from the doorway of the house: 'Har-veeee!'"

—in THE ABSENT-MINDED MURDERER by Cornell Woolrich

# Chapter IV

---

# Resonance

---

We have already noted (Chapter 1) that sound generated at the vocal bands is only the beginning of voice, so tiny in amount that it cannot be heard, and that it must be amplified many times before it reaches the ear of the listener. At this stage of voice production let us compare it to a phonograph. Obviously, if we put a record on the turntable and disconnect the speaker, no sound will fill the room. However, if we listen with one ear close to the tone arm, we can hear the music flow in such a tiny stream of sound that it seems like an elfin orchestra playing and a fairy singing. Only after the speaker is connected and the sound is amplified in the horn will it become audible in the room. Furthermore, given a good recording, the quality of the speaker will largely determine the quality of the sounds we should hear. Just so, given healthy vocal bands in the human instrument, strong and well controlled breathing muscles, the quality of the voice will depend finally on resonance.

## RESONANCE CHAMBERS HAVE WALLS OF BONE

A look at any musical instrument will show that the largest part of it is a hollow cavity of a certain size and shape. This is the resonance chamber for amplifying the sound. The human instrument, however, has several amplifying chambers within the body, which, for resonating purposes, is similar to the speaker box of a high fidelity phonograph housing several individual cones—"tweeters" and "woofers"—of varying sizes to amplify the full range of pitch vibrations. Each human being has a number of "woofers" and "tweeters" in connection with his own musical instrument to amplify the vocal sounds he generates.

In enumerating them let us begin with the lowest and largest, the chest cavity with its sympathetically vibrating walls of bone and muscle:

the rib cage, the sternum bone and the spinal column.* Above the chest, in the neck, at the top of the trachea lies the larynx itself, where voice is generated. Above the larynx is the pharynx. This is a hollow cavity behind the uvula with walls of pliable muscle. The pharynx is backed by the top of the spinal column. Then in the head we may note the smaller nasal cavities and higher up still the tiny sinus cavities set in the bones of the skull. Finally, the most important of all the resonance chambers, because it is the most flexible and controllable, is the oral cavity (the mouth). This chamber has the arched sounding board of the hard palate over it, the bony jaws and the teeth around it to act as sympathetic vibrators amplifying the sounds that pass through it. Note that every cavity offering resonance to the voice has walls of bone, hard muscle or cartilage; these bony walls of the chest and head all vibrate sympathetically and reinforce the original waves of sound generated in the larynx.

## WAVES OF SOUND SPREAD IN ALL DIRECTIONS

With our own body "woofers" and "tweeters" in mind let us see how they work. The sound waves started by the vibrating vocal bands spread in all directions exactly as waves generated by a pebble thrown into a quiet pool spread in concentric circles to the boundaries of the pool, or until the force generated by the dropped pebble has been dissipated.

We know that the waves of sound vary in length depending upon the pitch of the initial sound: the higher the pitch, the shorter its wave length and the faster its vibration; the lower the pitch, the longer the wave length and the slower the vibration. We have noted that there are empty resonance chambers of varying sizes from the large chest cavity to the tiny resonance chambers that act as amplifiers to the voice. It would seem obvious that the rapid, high-pitch sound waves, short in length, would be lost in the huge chest cavity, and that the long, low-pitch waves could not even enter the tiny "tweeters" of the mask of the face. We may conclude, then, that the various pitch vibrations of the voice are *amplified each in its appropriately-sized resonance chamber*. Each original sound wave entering its own resonance chamber sets up in the bony walls of the chamber sympathetic vibrations of overtones which reinforce and amplify the original sound.

---

*See Fig. 1, p. 9. It is argued that the space in the chest, filled as it is with spongy lungs and heart, is limited too much for resonance. But there is no doubt about the sympathetic vibrations of the low keys set up in the walls of the chest. One need only to place the hand on the back of a speaker to feel the vibrations in the bones under his hand.

It is not difficult to realize that for good resonance, the various resonance chambers must be open and free: the chest held high, not caved in on the lungs and heart and filling up whatever space might remain for resonance of the low keys. The outer muscles of the throat and neck must be relaxed, not pulled in to pinch the trachea and larynx. Similarly, the walls of the pharynx must not constrict too tightly lest they reduce the size of that cavity. The much smaller head chambers of the nasal and sinus cavities must also be kept open and clear. One has often heard the effect on vocal quality of noses and sinuses stopped up with colds and infections. Finally, to insure good oral resonance, it is important to learn the technique of articulation with flexible tongue and freely moving jaw and lips. These techniques in respect to the full use of the oral chamber will be discussed in detail in Chapters 7, 8, 9 and 10 in connection with the study of vowels.

## TO SUMMARIZE

As we have seen, effective voice production is dependent first upon an evenly controlled, smoothly flowing breath stream which passes through the closed glottis and sets the vocal bands in vibration. The outgoing breath stream carries sound waves which radiate in concentric circles, setting up sympathetic vibrations in the bony walls of the cavities within the chest and head. These cavities amplify the original sound until it is clearly audible and put a final stamp of quality on it.

In each step of voice production, the last no less than the first, careful controls over the operation of every piece of apparatus involved must become habitual. The various control techniques are all inextricably bound up together, and are dependent so largely upon the fundamental control over the techniques of breathing that we shall devote the final chapter in Part I to the problem of breath control.

❋        ❋        ❋

"The young girl's voice was like a clear dew drop, sweet and fresh, but so delicate and small that one feared a strong north wind would chill it to death."

—by a student

# GLOSSARY

## RESONANCE

| DESIRABLE | UNDESIRABLE |
|---|---|

1. *FREE ORAL RESONANCE.* The voice seems to "fall forward to a focus," clear, resonant and well projected. Under the arch of the palate all sympathetic vibrations are welded into one focused tone.

"At the height of his powers his voice was a superb musical instrument with never a 'wolf' tone through all the register. ___ ___ in volume it rose to thunder stm ___ ___ ___ the ears, a thirty-two foot diapason, not a foghorn . . ."
—of W. J. Bryan in
INCREDIBLE TALES
    by Gerald W. Johnson

"His voice had that three-dimensional quality: length, width and depth. His rich tone brought forth well-rounded ___ vibrating through the air as though ___ ___ standing on a mountain, and I hearing clear strong echo."
        —by a student

2. *WARM NASAL RESONANCE.* A warm musical quality is overlaid upon the strong, fundamental vocal stream issuing from the oral cavity. The sound waves of the higher overtones, have set up sympathetic vibrations in the frontal bones of the head, especially in the nasal turbinate bones.

1. *SQUEEZED PHARYNGEAL RESONANCE.* A harshness and a hoarse edginess make this a hard voice, grating on the ears of listeners. The voice seems to be held prisoner in the pharynx or dropped down the throat. The muscles of the soft palate, of the throat, and even the larger muscles of the neck are constricted and tight. Further, these constrictions reduce the size of the "open door" into the mouth from the pharynx, and so ___ ___ with the forward movement of the v___ ___ ___ and through the important oral resonance chamber.

"His voice when he spoke, and especially when he raised it in preaching, was harsh like the grating of iron hinges when a seldom used door is opened."
—in CHROME YELLOW
        by Aldous Huxley

___ ___ came from a throat of sandpaper. it ___ ___ if her neck muscles were busy sanding down her vocal bands."
        —by a student

2a. *SHARP NASALITY.* A piercing sharpness, high in pitch, often whining and most unpleasant. The vocalized breath stream has gone up into the nose instead of forward through the mouth. This may be a matter of interfering muscles which should be relaxed during speech, the walls at the back of the mouth pulling

"Ful wel she sang the service
  divine,
Intoned in her nose ful semely."
—of the Nun in
CANTERBURY TALES
        by Geoffrey Chaucer

"At last a soft and solemn-
  breathing sound
Rose like a stream of rich dis-
  tilled perfumes
And stole upon the air . . . . .
. . . . . . . . . . but o' ere long
Too well I did perceive it was
  the voice
Of my most honored lady, your
  dear sister.
—in COMUS
        by John Milton

"Her warm and comforting
voice produced the same effect
that a well-heated room would
have on a traveler who had
walked a mile on a cold and
bitter night."
                —by a student

together, taut and hard, closing
the entrance into the mouth
from the throat. Or it may be
just plain bad habit of "speaking through the nose" carried
over from childhood, a habit
gained through whining atti-
tudes or other emotionalisms.
Certainly a lazy inattention to
vocal quality is indicated and a
lack of control over the direction of the vocal stream forward
through the oral chamber where
articulation should take place.

"An actor with . . . a voice
which was dependent so much
upon the resonance of a cavern-
ous nose that it was a . . . highly
cultivated neigh."
—of Henry Irving in the Preface by G. B. Shaw, in ELLEN
  TERRY AND BERNARD
  SHAW: A CORRESPOND-
  ENCE
        by Christopher St. John

2b. *HEADY HUM.* A heavy humming tone surrounds the fundamental tone and obscures clarity. The voice seems to float
  around in the head without
  finding egress, except what
  might sift down through the
  nose.

"His voice seemed to originate
somewhere high in the back of
his head, and to emerge, finally, through his nostrils; it was
like a ceaseless hum of some
articulate bee."
—of Amos Force in
THE LAST HURRAH
        by Edwin O'Connor

3. *DEEP CHEST RESONANCE.* A voice with enough low keys in its range to insure a deep, vibrant warmth, a soft, velvety tone. The vibrating waves of low-keyed sounds have set up sympathetic vibrations in the bony walls of the chest. The voice must not, however, be overwhelmed by a heavy, low-keyed rumbling which would obscure articulation of vowels in the oral chamber.

"When she spoke, her voice had a beautiful low timbre, soft and modulated, yet with ringing overtones."
—in GRAPES OF WRATH
by John Steinbeck

". . . a low voice, in which a vibrant wire was thrumming . ."
—of Mrs. Leonard in
LOOK HOMEWARD, ANGEL
by Thomas Wolfe

3. *HEAVY INDISTINCT RUMBLE.* A low rumbling tone without focused clarity, resembling an animal growl more than human articulation. There is always the deep, very low key, rarely any use of the middle or higher pitch. The chest resonance so predominates as to obscure frontal or oral resonance. The speaker with this heavy, rumbling voice rarely moves his jaw or lips in speaking.

". . . then that of a heavy, deep one—the thickest sounding voice I had ever heard. It had a clabbery quality, too, as though it came bubbling up from under water."
—of Major Roger in
NORTHWEST
by Kenneth Roberts

4. *WELL BALANCED RESONANCE.* A clear, warm sonorous voice using a variety of keys from low to high with consequent chest, oral and nasal resonance blended together under the sounding board of the palate as articulation takes place.

"Instantly distinguishable from all others, there was a single all-pervading, all-compelling, all-inclusive and all-dominating voice . . . It was distinguished by a perfectly astounding richness and indescribable sonority that semed to have in it the compacted resonance in the

4. *LACK OF RESONANCE.* "A monstrous little voice," faint, dry, seemingly far away, colorless and usually monotonous, with a small range of pitch and very little force.

"So entirely had it lost the life and resonance of the human voice that it affected the senses like a once beautiful color faded away into a poor weak stain. So sunken and depressed it was, that it was like a voice underground."

—of Dr. Manette in
A TALE OF TWO CITIES
by Charles Dickens

voice of every Irishman who ever lived,—this magnificently full-bodied voice of Celtic richness."
—of Seamus Malone in
THE WEBB AND THE ROCK
       by Thomas Wolfe

"Anon, his voice appeared to fill the air yet not with an obtrusive clangor. The sound was of a murmurous character, soft, attractive, persuasive, friendly. The sound had its pathos, too."
—from THE MARBLE FAUN
       by Nathaniel Hawthorne

"His voice was like a little frayed ribbon fluttering pointlessly in the air."
—of an old Oriental in
SEVEN WHO FLED
       by Frederik Prokosch

"A voys he hadde so small as hath a goat."
—of the Pardoner in
CANTERBURY TALES
       by Geoffrey Chaucer

❁   ❁   ❁

"His voice had a weird, far-away sound. It sounded as though he were whispering through a megaphone and, although he was close by, you felt he was speaking from another part of the world."

—by a student

## THE VOICE OF THE POET COLERIDGE

"Mr. Coleridge rose and gave out his text: 'And he went up into the mountain to pray, Himself, alone.' As he gave out this text his voice 'rose like a stream of rich perfumes,' and when he came to the last two words which he pronounced loud, deep and distinct, it seemed to me, who was then young, as if the sounds had echoed from the bottom of the human heart, and as if that prayer might have floated in solemn silence through the universe."

—William Hazlitt writing on Milton's COMUS

## Chapter V

# Breath Control

It is the vocal shades and tones of the speaker that put the final stamp of significance and subtlety to the meaning of the words he utters. The techniques for this are dependent upon four aspects of control over the outgoing breath stream, each of which has an immediate effect on phonation and resonance and even on articulation. Vocal quality and effectiveness of speaking, therefore, are vitally affected by these controls. Conversely, the loss of control of any one of them has also an immediate result in poor communication. These four breath controls are: (1) control over the *amount* of breath released in exhalation, (2) control over the *attack* on the vocal bands; (3) control over the *flow* of the breath stream; (4) control over the *direction* of the exhaled breath stream on its way out of the body. At this point we suggest that you review Chapter 2—Breathing.

## THE AMOUNT OF EXHALED BREATH

During speech one single stream of utterance with meaning and significance should correspond to one single stream of breath. As we group our thoughts and words for meaningful expression inhalation and exhalation should be planned accordingly. The amount of breath and voice needed is determined not only by the length of the word group, but also by the kind and degree of emotion in it and by the volume or force needed for its expression. From beginning to end of the word group there must be an equal amount of breath support under the tone and volume of voice. Too much breath, however, must not be released at the beginning of utterance leaving so little breath to finish the sentence that the voice "runs down" and "peters out" at the end. An adequate stream of sound from beginning to end of a word group can be assured only by sufficient inhalation.

Everything about the breath is the direct result of the movement of the muscles involved in breathing. To regulate the amount of breath generating a stream of voice calls for a practiced control over these muscles: i.e., over the extent and rate of the movement of the diaphragm and the simultaneous actions of the upper abdominal and intercostal muscles. The action of the outer muscles of the abdomen in the region of the waistline may be seen and felt (p. 9, Chapter 2). This being so, control over them is comparatively simple to acquire by the persistent use of the exercises in Part I of the *Work Book* and the passages in Part I of the *Practice Reading Book*.

## THE BREATH ATTACK ON THE VOCAL BANDS

The second problem of breath control has to do with the initial charge of breath upon the vocal bands, setting them in vibration. The vocal bands are very delicate and sensitive, and for ordinary speech the breath should attack them easily and gently, yet firmly, but not suddenly nor violently. The force of the breath generating sound is determined by the force or movement of the breathing muscles. The force of the breath is therefore controlled by controlling the force of movement of these muscles. As you work for breath controls, center your attention on the actions taking place in the region of the waistline. See that there is a definite expansion upon inhalation, then feel the muscles reverse themselves and contract smoothly and slowly under your carefully imposed control as the breath is exhaled. With deliberate practice involuntary habits can be set up of smoothly coordinated actions of these muscles, making it possible to have a controlled breath stream generating a controlled vocal stream ready at all times to meet the demands of expressive speaking.

## THE FLOW OF BREATH

Once the attack has been made on the vocal bands and sound generated, the vocalized breath stream must continue to flow smoothly and evenly. However, there should not only be enough breath for equal distribution of voice, but the voice should increase or diminish smoothly under the speaker's control to meet the varied demands of expression, just as a singer must be able to crescendo or diminuendo smoothly. While control over the continuous flow of breath throughout utterance is closely connected with control over the amount of breath, we must be able, also, to increase or decrease the force and rate of exhalation for an increase or decrease of volume as desired.

Another aspect of this problem is to see that the flow of voice is smooth and firm, not wobbly and uneven. Only a balanced stance with the weight evenly distributed on both feet, and a straight posture will insure a smooth, evenly flowing voice. To "stand up straight" is necessary to allow an even pull of the diaphragmatic muscles which, as we have seen, govern the flow of breath, and hence the flow of tone. If you stand with your weight shifted to your left foot, leg, hip, for instance, then the left hip will be higher than the right, and the pull of the diaphragmatic muscles over the hips will be uneven with one side taut and the other lax. Inhalation and exhalation will then be unsteady and uncontrolled. It is important, therefore, that you stand evenly balanced on both feet as you do the exercises in the *Work Book* and read the passages in the *Reading Book*. It becomes more and more clear that breathing exercises are basic to all vocal development.

## THE DIRECTION OF THE BREATH

also control over the direction of its flow after it passes through the glottis and has generated voice. Breath now becomes the carrier of the voice, as it were, proceeding first from the larynx to the pharynx. From the pharynx there are two passageways by which the stream of air may find its way out of the body. In silent breathing, it flows up into the nasal passages, then down and out through the nose; but in speaking it should move forward through the oral chamber and out. In other words, here is a choice to make requiring a mental, voluntary control over the direction of the voice. This choice of direction is important to the quality of the resonance of the voice and of the articulation of American speech. For good and desirable quality of voice and speech it is fundamental primary, vocalized breath stream go forward through the oral chambers.

Implicit in this control is the importance of the relaxation of the muscles of swallowing in the soft walls at the back of the mouth, that is, of the soft palate and the uvula. If these muscles tighten and harden, they can almost close the entrance into the mouth from the pharynx, and the vocalized breath stream will then go up into the nasal passage rather than forward into the oral chamber. The relaxation and non-use of these swallowing muscles during speech must be ensured.

Mainly, however, control over the direction of the vocalized breath is a thought control and must be imposed consciously during the training period. The vocalized breath stream should be deliberately sent forward through the mouth. After a time of consistent, conscious control over the direction of the breath, the flow of tone through the oral chamber, insuring desirable oral resonance, will become habitual, and involuntary controls will take over.

## TO SUMMARIZE

The desirable qualities of voice and speech are all basically dependent upon controls over the exhaled breath stream. Conversely, the lack of breath controls in any one of its phases results in undesirable qualities and prevents effective communication. It cannot be said too often, that of all the muscles involved in speaking, control over the muscles of breathing is fundamental. Voluntary control is necessary through a period of exercise and practice in order to establish desirable habits of involuntary control. Throughout the training period it must be remembered that the action of these muscles determines the *amount* and *rate* and *force* of exhalation, which in turn determines the strength of vibration of the vocal bands. The smooth, even flexibility of their vibration sets up sound waves rippling into all the empty, cove-like chambers of the head which offer resonance to the voice and quality of tone for expressive communication. Controls must be established over the amount of breath used for utterance, over the "attack" upon the vocal bands initiating voice, over the continued generating of voice evenly and smoothly to the end of utterance and, finally, over the direction of that vocal stream for the most desirable quality of resonance, oral clarity.

❀      ❀      ❀

"I can still hear that cry, as for twenty mornings long I heard it close behind me, breathy, full-throated, hideously stressed, with a harsh open *e*, uttered in accents of mechanical despair. 'Fuggiero! Rispondi almendo! Answer when I call you!'"

—from MARIO AND THE MAGICIAN by Thomas Mann

# GLOSSARY

## BREATH CONTROL

| *DESIRABLE* | *UNDESIRABLE* |
|---|---|

1. *JUST ENOUGH BREATH* to vibrate the vocal bands gently and produce a clear voice of adequate strength to be heard easily; a minimal amount of air flowing through the tiny slit of the glottis to create a sufficient amount of sound. (See Glossary, Chapter 1, Description 4.)

"Her sweet speech, much more sweet than the murmuring of a slow stream, which breaks its way among the little rocks, or ~~~ ~~~~~~~ ~~ the breeze amongst the leaves.

—in AMINTO, by Tasso (Translation by Ernest Grillo.)

1a. *TOO MUCH BREATH* produces a breathy quality of voice with no clear tone, or a heavily husky, raspy, or wheezy voice. (See Glossary, Chapter 1, Description 1; also, Glossary, Chapter 3, Description 1.) The unnecessary force of air rasps the vocal bands, creating a grating, scratchy sound; or the air escapes through a too wide opening of the glottis and surrounds the speech with breathiness. (See Glossary, Chapter 3, Description 3.)

"The whispery breathings of ~~~ voice surrounded her listeners like a dense, close, white fog."

—by a student

1b. *TOO LITTLE BREATH* produces a weak, whispery voice with very little force and little carrying power. (See Glossary, Chapter 1, Description 4.) The breathing muscles act with the least amount of energy, and so little air passes through the glottis that there is hardly enough force to vibrate the vocal bands.

"The faintness of the voice was pitiable and dreadful. It was not the faintness of physical weakness, though confinement and hard fare had their part. Its deplorable peculiarity was that it was the faintness of solitude and disuse. It was like the last, feeble echo of a sound made long, long ago."

—of Dr. Manette in
TALE OF TWO CITIES
by Charles Dickens

2. *EASY ATTACK.* Speech begins easily, a gentle breathing into sound. After inhalation, the breathing muscles reverse their actions easily, slowly, evenly, so that breath passes between the vocal bands at the same gentle, slow pace, with the same gentle force as the muscles act. (See Glossary, Chapter 3, description 1.)

"It was so easy, so natural, so pure, and so unforced, that she had only to open her mouth and the miracle occurred . . . She could dominate you just because of her voice, or even the memory of her voice."

—of Irela in EVENSONG
by Beverly Nichols

2. *VIOLENT ATTACK.* The voice seems to explode from the speaker in forced, harsh, and husky tones. Muscle actions for exhalation are sudden and more or less violent, and breath seems to assault the vocal bands fiercely. (See also Glossary, Chapter 3, Description 1.)

"He cried aloud, and there was a note in his voice that reminded Samuel of some wild old lioness roaring to her young. . . . He understood now why they called him 'Sounding Sea.'"

—of Tai Haruru in
GREEN DOLPHIN STREET
by Elizabeth Goudge

"All his words were spoken on the same key, and each sentence seemed like another blast of a fog horn, so near it made one jump."

—by a student

3. *SMOOTH AND EVEN FLOW.* A flow of voice that is even and steady from the beginning to the end of sentences or word groups as a result of a steady, gentle flow of breath through the glottis. The great breathing muscles act with an evenly distributed force and a slow movement, producing a steady stream of exhaled breath, just enough to generate a steady stream of clear voice with firm support under it. (See Glossary, Chapter 3, Description 2.)

3. *UNSTEADY, TREMULOUS VOICE.* The voice seems actually to wobble and waver, to quiver and quaver. There is no firm breath support under it. The pull of the diaphragmatic muscles in contraction and relaxation is uneven, tighter on one side than on the other, due, usually, to an unbalanced posture, or to weakness. The muscle movements being unsteady, the flow of breath through the glottis will be unsteady. Consequently, the voice will be un-

"Then whatever she had decided she made known in a few simple, clear words, her voice always pretty and smooth and gentle as water slipping over stones."
—of Mme. Wu in
PAVILION OF WOMEN
by Pearl Buck

4. *G R A D U A L  C R E S C E N D O AND DECRESCENDO.* The breathing muscles gradually increase the rate and force of their movements on exhalation, and the exhaled breath increases in force and movement to the ~~same~~ degree with corresponding crescendo ~~— — — For a~~ decrescendo the muscles slow down in movement and force, lessening the volume and power of the voice at the same rate.

"Then a low deep sound was heard like the suppressed accompaniment of distant music, rising just high enough on the air to be audible. . . . It was, however, succeeded by another ~~and — —— strain~~ . . . until they grew on the ear, ~~——~~ long-drawn and often repeated interjections, and finally in words. The strains rose just so loud as to be intelligible, and then grew fainter and more trembling, until they finally sank on the ear, as if borne away by a passing breath of wind."
—from **THE LAST OF THE MOHICANS**
by James Fennimore Cooper

"She began softly, as though speaking to herself of emotions of utmost privacy, a sound not steady and fluttery, rather than smooth-flowing and firm.

"As if it took all her energy to produce, her voice fluttered between her lips as wispy and delicate as a spider's web between two branches of a lilac bush."
—by a student

4a. *SUDDEN LOUDNESS.* The voice is suddenly very loud with forced breathiness surrounding it. The breathing muscles during exhalation are suddenly and quickly tightened; air, in consequence, moves out through the glottis with the same sudden and quickened force.

"~~When reading~~ aloud his voice played ~~staggering~~ ~~— —~~ him, now almost too soft to hear, now blaring like a foghorn."
—of Lawrence Palinode in
MORE WORK FOR THE UNDERTAKER
by Margery Allingham

"He sounded like the ocean with the rush, swoop and noise of his voice."
—by a student

4b. *RUNS DOWN, "P E T E R S OUT."* There is plenty of tone and volume at the beginning of a word group, but the voice loses both tone and volume rapidly as it goes on to the end of a sentence. After expansion of the breathing muscles for inhalation, the reverse action is too fast, and the air moves out of the lungs with a rush, like air out of a deflating balloon.

addressed to the gathering but which they overheard almost against her will. Gradually she increased its volume, until at times the voice seemed to become a dissembled force shaking her as though it had become the source of her being rather than the fine spun web of her own creation."

—In THE INVISIBLE MAN, by Ralph Elison

Passing through the glottis, it initiates a strong voice which quickly loses power and energy as the lungs rapidly empty. Exhalation after shallow inhalation by the shoulder-raising method (clavicular breathing; see Glossary, Chapter 2, Description 1.) nearly always results in a "petering out" of voice before the end of a word group.

"Suddenly she would blare out, 'I want you to . . .' But Jimmy never knew what his mother wanted, for her voice always ran down into a toneless mumble before she ever got to the important part of her sentence."

—by a student

5. *FORWARD PLACEMENT.* A well projected voice of good carrying power. The fundamental, vocalized breath stream has been directed forward from the pharynx into the oral chamber and out into space through the doorway of the lips; the result of deliberately and willfully "thinking" the voice forward from the pharynx, instead of allowing it to rise into the nasal passageway and the tiny cavities of the head.

"He spoke in a quiet, confidential half-tone, but every word was distinctly audible in the last row of the balcony. He

5a. *BACK PLACEMENT.* A throaty, harsh, constricted voice with little power. The fundamental, vocalized breath stream is held back and down in the throat; it is not allowed to move forward freely into the mouth, and thence out to the ears of the listeners. (See Glossary, Chapter 4, Description 1.)

"His voice sounded hoarse and awkward, like a rusty lock."
—of Ben Gunn in
TREASURE ISLAND
by Robert Louis Stevenson

"The old woman spoke in a thin whine that sounded like a voice

---

*William Jennings Bryan (Glossary, Chapter 2, Description 1; Chapter 4, Description 1.) must have used this technique of forward focus to have had the volume and carrying power in his voice for which he was noted. Ellen Terry (Glossary, Chapter 1, Description 4), as George Bernard Shaw described her "slightly veiled voice" which "reached the listeners in the theatre without any apparent effort," must also have employed this technique.

seemed to have the power of projecting sound straight from his lips to the ear of the listener; he kept his chin high and his words went out into the audience instead of dribbling down his shirt front."

—by a student

on a shortwave broadcast under bad atmospheric conditions; it had some kind of bronchial static in it. She muttered and cackled like an old-fashioned crystal receiver."

—in THE WALL
by John Hersey

5b. *HEAD-CONFINED.* A voice that is either pinched and piercing, the fundamental vocalized breath stream caught in a cul-de-sac; or a voice that is indistinct and inarticulate, drowned in a heady humming vibration, the fundamental stream of sound floating into the head cavities "up under the eaves." (See Glossary, Chapter 4, Description —,

"Her voice lives in her sinuses, and is as small, defiant and girlish as her nose."
—of Helinka, in THE WALL,
by John Hersey

"Her voice was like a mewing cat, slightly high-pitched, carefully spaced in little rhythmic stresses and so soft that one had to strain to hear her."
—by a student

❁   ❁   ❁

". . . Then I noticed Patricia's curious manner of speech. She used her voice as people do whose conversation must not be overheard: prisoners, patrol leaders, hunters. It was a secret neutral voice, devoid of resonance; somehow it conveyed a quality of silence."

—in THE LION by Joseph Kessel
translated from the French by Peter Green

"Her voice was sweet and smooth as taffy and one could almost see the melted sugar surrounding the words as they dropped from her lips."

—by a student

# PART II - SOUND AND SENSE

## Voice and Articulation

\* \* \*

"You are silent. . . . You do not live the Word, or you are charry with it to unfriendliness. The articulate world does not know where it is with you. My friend, that is perilous, Speech is civilization itself. The word, even the most contradictious word, preserves contact—it is silence which isolates."

—from THE MAGIC MOUNTAIN by Thomas Mann

"Music had stirred him like that. Music had troubled him many times. But music was not articulate. . . . Words! Mere words! How terrible they were! How clear, and vivid, and cruel! One could not escape from them. And yet what a subtle magic there was in them! They seemed to be able to give a plastic form to formless things, and to have a music of their own as sweet as that of viol or of lute. Mere words! Was there anything so real as words?"

—from THE PICTURE OF DORIAN GRAY
by Oscar Wilde

# Chapter VI

## Speech

"Consonants give intelligibility to speech, but vowels give beauty of utterance. Consonants constitute the backbone of spoken language—vowels the flesh and blood. You cannot do without them."

—Alexander Graham Bell

All the vertebrate animals can make sounds which seem to make sense to others of their kind. The mating call of the bull moose, we are told is an awesome thing. Parakeets, parrots and macaws, and even crows, can be taught to imitate the syllables of men, but only man can train himself to make an infinite variety of aural effects and weave meanings into a vast and complex tapestry of sounds. Indeed man did not become truly human until he developed spoken language, according to one sociologist.*

For millennia, doubtless, man communicated much as animals do, developing through time more complex codes of communication with nods and gestures, by painting pictures on rocks, drawing pictures in the sand, cutting figures into stone, by ceremonial dancing, and at long last in particularized vocal syllables. The making of the particularized sounds of the language, the combining of them into syllables and the syllables into words is ARTICULATION. Then EXPRESSIVENESS, which adds fuller significance to the meaning of articulated words, is the third dimension in effective speaking. The whole concept of oral communication—the making, the receiving, the understanding of vocal sound—is rather amusingly put in Gerald DuMaurier's novel, *Peter Ibbetson*: "You fill your lungs with wind and shake a little slit in your throat, and make mouths, and that shakes the air; and the air shakes a pair of little drums in my head—a very complicated arrangement, with lots of bones behind—and my brain seizes your meaning in the rough."**

*"The Language of Nods" by Stuart Chase in THE SATURDAY REVIEW, March 2, 1957, p. 18.
**Published by Harper Brothers.

Up to now we have been concentrating on the study of voice as an instrument and the acquiring of techniques for playing that instrument to produce clear and flexible vocal tone. At this point it would be well to remind ourselves that the study of voice is not an end in itself, but only the first step in the long-range purpose of our study—to gain those physical techniques which will improve our powers of oral communication.

That being the case, to the training of the great muscles of breathing and the muscles operating the vocal bands themselves, we must now add the training of those muscles affecting articulation if we would add easily understood sense to clear sounds. FIGURE 7 is a diagram of the

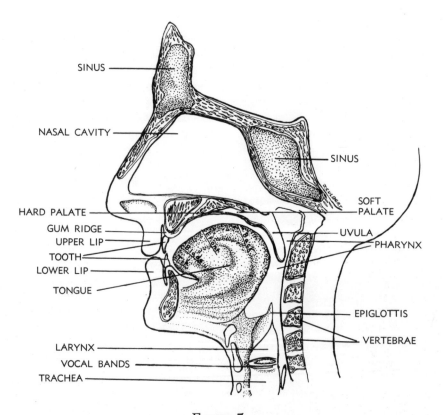

FIGURE 7

THE ORGANS OF SPEECH WITH THE HEAD RESONATORS.

SPEECH TRACT. Note not only the larynx and vocal bands that produce voice, but more particularly the organs of articulation: the movable jaw, the tongue which is capable of amazing flexibility, the hard palate, and the lips which are capable of much variation in shape. Note also the resonating factors: the several chambers of the pharynx, the nasal cavity and sinuses, and the most important oral chamber, along with the numerous bones of the head, which offer sympathetic vibrations of the original vocal vibrations. (Chapter IV)

To gain good techniques of voice production is largely a problem of developing muscular strength and control of the breathing muscles. To gain effective techniques of speech is mainly a problem of developing fine flexibility of the muscles of articulation, especially of the tongue, with controlled and flexible movements of the jaw and lips.

In PART II, then, we shall give attention in partciular to the enunciation of the individual sounds of American speech and the pronunciation of words as used by educated people. Since there seems to be a variable and inconstant relationship between spelling and pronunciation in the English language, a phonetic alphabet for each speech sounds would be a great help in our study.* Obviously the first person who identifies a written symbol with its sound by pronouncing it to you in key words will fix that symbol with that sound in your ears. Undoubtedly that person will be your speech teacher; but there will be an array of other teachers who may vary the pronunciation of the same key words.

At this point you may wish that there were some sure and rigid standard of speech† by which you could identify the individual sounds with exactitude. But, on second thought, if there were such a rigid standard we would lose much of the picturesque and colorful in American speech. Fortunately for the sake of better understanding, local deviations from the general pattern are becoming less and less pronounced among cultured people. While it is true that there is no absolute standard of pronunciation in America and that local usage plays a large role in the speech pattern of the country, yet there is a flexible

---

*The diacritical markings used by lexicographers are a simplified pronunciation guide for the everyday use of the layman, but they fall far short of the range and precision we shall need and shall find in the International Phonetic Alphabet (IPA). However, because familiarity with at least one of these systems is, of course, necessary, Chapters of Part II will show, alongside the IPA, the diacritical marking system (DMS) used in Webster's New International Dictionary, Third Edition, 1961.

†H. L. Menken in his monumental work, THE AMERICAN LANGUAGE, has a lively account of several attempts to legislate into existence an American standard of speech.

standard pretty generally agreed upon which can be discovered by
turning to any dictionary. But it is more important to realize that there
is a *high standard of speech based on certain universally accepted
qualities.* As you try to discover those standards by listening to people
speak, ask yourself these questions:

1. Are the vowels enunciated with clarity and unmistakable dis-
   tinctiveness?
2. Is there neatness and deftness in enunciation of the consonants
   that break up the vowel stream and create syllables?
3. Are the syllables spoken flexibly and smoothly with a nice relationship of strong and weak syllables?

If you hear these qualities of speech, then listen to them. Capture them
on the sound track of your memory and repeat them over and over
again, imitating your model of good speech as accurately as you can.

## VOWELS ARE THE VOICE

Chapter 4, RESONANCE, put considerable emphasis on the oral
chamber as the most important of the resonance chambers. Chapter 5,
BREATH CONTROL, laid stress on sending the vocalized breath
stream forward through the oral chamber. Now, in this section, the
oral chamber is again the focal point of attention, for it is here that
all verbal distinctions are formed. Within the mouth we are able to make
a great number of individually shaped and differently sized resonance
chambers, each of which results in an altogether different and distinctive sound when voice flows through it. These resonant vocal sounds,
particularized patterns of voice, are the vowel sounds of any language.
*Vowels,* then, *are the voice.* At this point the study of oral resonance
for good vocal clarity and the study of vowels for clear articulation
come together. The correct forming of vowels, important as they are
to articulate clarity, will also improve the quality of the voice by en-
suring highly desirable oral resonance.

As we have indicated, any vowel sound is the immediate result of
voice sent through a particular resonance chamber formed in the oral
cavity by the movements of the lower jaw, the tongue and the lips.
Indeed, if the jaw, tongue and lips of a speaker were suddenly to lock
in the position of uttering a vowel sound—"ah," for instance—he could
make no other sound until those organs of speech should be unlocked
and move into a different position. He might sing a merry tune with

that vowel sound, changing pitch, pace and rhythm, but he could not alter in the least the articulated sound itself. Let there be, however, the slightest movement of the tongue, or of the jaw, or of the lips, and the sound changes in identity and character in midstream, as it were. This is demonstrated in the vocal exercise that starts with a hum and opens into a full "ah" sound. (p. 37 *Work Book*, Part I.) Then, as the mouth closes gradually, the sound changes slowly back again, moving from the open "ah" sound through less and less open sounds until the lips are again closed in the original hum.

As we proceed toward our goal of effective communication we must realize that we cannot drop all thought of Part I and the practice of good voice production, as we now give our attention to Part II. On the contrary in Part II we are investing voice with articulate sense, making sense out of sound. Our concern now is how to give the general quality of voice a particular distinction, an articulate neatness and significance of enunciation. Since the vowels are the particulars of the voice in speaking, we shall give them our first consideration.

## CONSONANTS ARE THE INTERRUPTIONS OF THE VOWEL STREAM

If vowels were the only sounds made by human beings in their efforts to communicate with each other, our language would be very limited as a means of communication. Such a limited language, for instance, is Hawaiian, or any other of the Polynesian group. The word *Hawaii* itself is a good example. Each of the last three vowels is a syllable ̩ ̩ ̩̩ ̩̩ ̩̩ ̩̩ ̩̩ there are no diphthongs in any of the Polynesian languages, and no vowel elision. Each vowel is ˉkicked out, as it were, ̩̩̩̩ ̩̩ glottal shock. Furthermore, there are only seven consonant sounds— *h, k, p, l, m, n,* and *w*—to our twenty-three or so.* If new words are needed to communicate a new idea, or a variant of an old one, the Polynesians duplicate syllables or even whole words. For example, the Hawaiian word for small is "lii"; to describe anything very small the Hawaiians say "liilii." In Maori the word "haere" (ha-ay-ray) means going; thus, "haerehaere" is to roam about, take a walk.†

With a flick of the tongue or a compression of the lips we can interrupt the vowel stream, either partially or completely, with one or

---

*Including combinations of consonants, as *ch* in *church, j* and *ge* in *judge.*
†Encyclopedia Britannica. 14th Ed. Vol. 18, p. 89; *Polynesian Languages.*

another of our twenty-three consonants and thus form a great number of different syllables. A syllable is a unit of utterance. It may be a lone vowel sound (a *sonant*) or a combination of a vowel and a consonant (a lesser or subordinate sonant, a *con-sonant*) which interrupts the flow of the vowel stream sufficiently to articulate another syllable of a different character.

## TO SUMMARIZE

We now add sense to the sound of the voice through the process of articulation, which is the interruption of the vowel stream by consonants, thus creating syllables. Oral communication is the pronunciation of the recognized syllables of the words of the language meaningfully put together. While there is no rigid standard of pronunciation imposed upon us here in America, there is a universal *standard of quality of enunciation*. This is based upon the particularity and neatness with which we articulate. To articulate neatly demands a flexibility and a control of the muscles of the organs of articulation: the tongue, the jaw, the lips.

✿   ✿   ✿

### A CONTRAST

"Slowly the rich music of his speech begins, each phrase scanned with clarifying emphasis, each word, each syllable given its noblest stature, sculptured in the round, each sibilant driven with the force of controlled power."

—John Gielgud's HAMLET
by Rosamond Gilder

"She clips her consonants with all the viciousness of a hound snapping at annoying flies. Each syllable is pronounced in the exaggerated manner of Eliza Doolittle learning her '*H*'."

—by a student

# GLOSSARY

## SPEECH

| *DESIRABLE* | *UNDESIRABLE* |
| --- | --- |

1. *GOOD GENERAL AMERI-CAN.* Fluent and unobtrusive speaking with pronunciation that is generally used by educated Americans across the country and enunciation that is easily understood.

"The pleasant musical quality of his voice is intensified by the clear, lustrous and distinct sounds of the vowels and consonants of the language, as he speaks in fluid cascades of words."

—by a student

1a. *PROVINCIAL, REGIONAL, DIALECTICAL.* Pronunciation and enunciation that is peculiar to a geographical section, or to a group of foreign-born, involving distortions of, substitutions for, and deviations from the vowels and consonants of good General American. Such distortions stand out and distract attention from the meaning.

" 'I knowed you wasn't Oklahomy folks. You talk queer kinda—That ain't no blame, you understan'. Everybody s a y s ˌ ˌˌˌ ·ˌ ˌ···ˌ ˌ··· 'Aˌ kansas folks says 'em differ'nt, an' Oklahomy folks says 'em differ'nt. An' we seen a lady from Massachusetts, an' she said 'em differ'ntest of all. Couldn't hardly make out what she was sayin'.' "

—from GRAPES OF WRATH, by John Steinbeck

1b. *PEDANTIC.* Over-precise correctness of articulation which calls attention to itself by its too-obvious virtues; lacks sincerity and natural fluency; borders on affectation.

"He enunciated and punctuated his words in such clear, precise tones and rhythmic patterns that in place of his face, I imagined an enormous clock with the hands moving steadily on, driven by a tick-tock, tick-tock pendulum inside his chest swinging unceasingly to and fro, to and fro, from one rib to another.

—by a student

2. *EASILY UNDERSTOOD.* Vowels are clear and particularized; consonants are clean and neat; each sonant and consonant having its proper amount and value of sound. The jaw, tongue and lips are flexible and free, functioning smoothly to create fluent sounds of language by which the listener catches meaning easily and quickly.

"His speech is most beautifully like sculpture — not a syllable slurred or scarred."

—of John Gielgud in *HAMLET* comment by Sydney Porter

"He has a clear, sharp manner of speaking. His words are crisply cut with the neatness of fine wood carving under a sharp chisel and the guiding mallet in the hands of an artist."

—of Walter Cronkite, Newscaster

—by a student

2. *SLOVENLY, CARELESS.* Vowels may be so little differentiated, or consonants so obtrusive or noisy, or lost altogether, that speech carries little meaning. The jaw moves little or with poor coordination; the tongue is sluggish; the teeth locked too close together, the lips stiff. There may be substitutes for and deviations from recognized vowel sounds; consonants may be dropped or thickened or substituted.

"He has a voice like thick soup, and speaks with the slovenly drawl of the new generation of Americans, dragging his words along like reluctant dogs on a string."

—of Greer in XINGU
   by Edith Wharton

"His speech was like a tangled chain; nothing impaired but all discorded."

—from MIDSUMMER NIGHT'S DREAM, Act V:1, by William Shakespeare

NOTE. Assignments I, I-A and I-B of the *Work Book* pp. 71, 73, 74 should be interesting and valuable to you at this point. You must develop a growing awareness of speech sounds to develop an effective standard in making them.

# Chapter VII

---

## Articulating the Vowels

---

A foreigner with a reading knowledge of English is almost hopelessly confused on hearing American English for the first time. On the printed page he *sees only five vowels* used over and over again to spell the words of the language, but he *hears twenty-four vowel sounds.* Often in the spelling of words he finds different combinations of the five cardinal vowels, which, he is told, are nevertheless pronounced as the ~~_____ 1. For example in~~ this sentence are four different spellings of the same vowel sound:

It's the *ear*ly b*ir*d that catches the f*ur*ry w*or*m.

On the other hand, he will find identical vowel combinations on the printed page, which, when read aloud, he will hear as completely different vowel sounds, as in this paragraph:

The hungry crow sat on the b*ough*\* of r*ough* bark above
the feeding tr*ough*, th*ough* his usual perch was in a tree
~~down by the slough~~. Back and forth along the b*ough*, c*ough*-
ing and cawing, he hopped w~~hile the pig~~ ~~_____~~
thr*ough* his mash in a thor*ough*ly gluttonous manner.

Consider these lines from an unknown verse maker on the same subject of English spelling and pronunciation, the relationship of which seems to have neither rhyme or reason:

When the English tongue we speak
Why is BREAK not rhymed with FREAK?
Will you tell me why it's true
We say SEW, but likewise FEW,

---

\*Just to complicate matters, the *gh* in these words has three different qualities of sounds: *f* in *cough* and *rough*; th (or f) in *trough;* silent in *through, though, bough, slough* and *thoroughly.*

And the maker of the verse
Cannot rhyme his HORSE with WORSE?
BEARD sounds not the same as HEARD;
CORD is different from WORD;
COW is COW, but LOW is LOW;
SHOE is never rhymed with FOE.
Think of HOSE, and DOSE and LOSE,
And of GOOSE and yet of CHOOSE.
Think of COMB and TOMB and BOMB,
DOLL and ROLL, and HOME and SOME,
And since pay is rhymed with say
Why not PAID with SAID, I pray?
We have BLOOD and FOOD, and GOOD;
MOULD is not pronounced like COULD.
Wherefore DONE, but GONE and LONE?
And, in short, it seems to me
Sounds and letters disagree.

                                             —Anon.

Although there are only five *vowel letters*, we recognize in good American speech fifteen distinct single *vowel sounds* and nine combinations of vowels called diphthongs. A diphthong is the sound of two vowels running quickly together in the same syllable, the jaw and tongue sliding smoothly from the position of the first, always the more open sound, into the second, the more closed sound. It is possible, of course, to make many more than these particular twenty-four sonants. Consider many foreign language sounds different from our own and certain deviations from the acceptable vowel sounds even among Americans. Sometimes these deviations are "hangovers" from foreign speech; sometimes they are vowel sounds peculiar to a locality. A Bostonian who flattens his *a*'s in an "ar" spelling will drop the *r* altogether and tell you that he "pa'ked his ca' on Pa'k Street"; a Texan knows "minny min who have tin million dollars;" a lass from Georgia wishes you a bright "Good mownin'"; while on that same morning in Brooklyn the truck driver on his coffee-break will complain bitterly: "This cawfee is awful. It's fu da boids an', tha's fu shir. Dey have a noive tu charge tsen cen's fu rit." Such sonant variations are indeed vowels, but they are *not the accepted vowel sounds* of the language as used by educated people of the country; nor do they come up to any standard of quality in the oral resonance of the voice and the particularity of enunciation of the sounds of the language.

As all vowel sounds are the immediate results of varying shapes and sizes of the resonance chambers created within the mouth, to articulate the correct and particular vowels of the language it will be necessary to put yourself through meticulous practice and drill. The same articulatory actions must be repeated until the muscles perform exactly so each time as a matter of habit, and the resulting vowel sounds will be exactly the same correct sounds each time.

## THE PCT IS THE KEY TO VOWELS

The jaw, the lips and the tongue are involved in forming vowels, as well as the palate to which the moving tongue comes into various degrees of proximity. That spot on the tongue which comes nearest to touching the palate, but without doing so, is called the PLACE OF CONSTRICTION OF THE TONGUE (the PCT), because at that point the tongue is constricted into a slight hump. Sometimes the PCT is high in the front of the mouth near the upper gum ridge; at another time it might be in the back and high near the soft palate; or again it might be low in the front or low in the back. ..... ... f... middle or back on the tongue, high, middle or low in relation to the palate—each position of the PCT determines a particular vowel sound.

Figure 8 is a diagram of the relative positions in the oral chamber for the making of the twenty-four English vowel sounds—fifteen single or "pure" vowels, and nine combinations, or diphthongs. On the diagram you will note the words FRONT, MIDDLE and BACK. These designations refer to those positions on the tongue where the PCT is nearest the front. middle or back of the palate. The vowels are called Front Vowels, Middle Vowels and Back Vowels ... ... .. li-b- The terms HIGH. HALF-HIGH, HALF-LOW and LOW likewise refer to the PCT in respect to its proximity to the palate. Suppose we put words into this "mouth." Read aloud the two sentences along the oblique lines, beginning with "She" and reading down the left (front vowel) line; then down the middle line. Begin the next sentence with "Carl" and read up the right (back vowel) line. As you read the sentences in Figure 8 word by word you will sound in succession each pure vowel as a result of constricting the tongue differently at each successive point in the mouth as indicated. Note that there are six such points on both the back and the front lines, and three on the middle line, indicating that for each vowel the PCT is at a different distance from the palate. Note particularly how each position produces a different vowel sound. It is plain to see that the PCT is

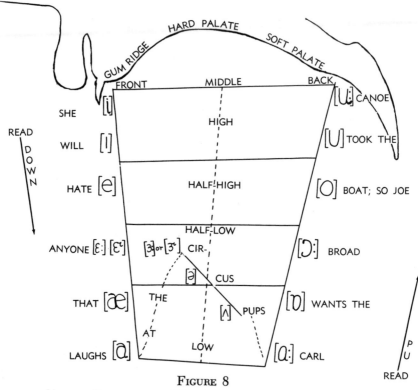

FIGURE 8

VOWEL CHART WITH IPA SYMBOLS AND KEY WORDS.
Diagram of relationships between tongue and palate when making
vowels and diphthongs.

the key to the making of vowels in any language and that flexibility of
the tongue is a necessity. Do Assignment III, p. 76 of the *Work Book*,
filling in the boxes with other key words.

## THE JAW AND THE LIPS MUST MOVE ALSO

Follow the chart of Figure 8 as you read these descriptions. While
the tongue may move vigorously in all its sections, flicking its tip,
or constricting at the front, middle or back, the oral chamber cannot
change size unless the jaw moves down. For each vowel in succession from high to low, the jaw drops open a little more enlarging the
chamber and pulling the lips a little farther apart.

Finally, there is a change of lip formation in the making of each vowel, also, which takes place simultaneously with the jaw and tongue movements and helps to shape each of the different vowel chambers. In general, the shape of the lips in making all front vowels is a horizontal ellipse. The lips are only slightly open for the high front vowel in "she," with the corners pulled back; they are much wider apart, with the corners still back, to make the low front vowel in "laugh." For the high back vowel in "canoe," however, the lips are tightly rounded and pursed; for the next two back vowels, in "took" and "boat" they are also rounded, though gradually more relaxed. With the half-low back vowel in "broad" the lips begin to open into a narrow vertical oval and are open in the same general oval shape, but growing wider, for the two low back vowels in "wants" and "Carl." In making the first middle vowel, the PCT is midway between the back and the front of the mouth; the tongue lies about midway between high and low, with the jaw and lips open about midway in a small oval.

A diphthong, which is composed of two vowels, involves an "off glide from the ~~—~~ Smoothly and flexibly the lips, jaw and tongue change position from the oral chamber of the first to form the oral chamber of the second. A vivid example is the simple word *how* [haʊ], because it involves the lowest and most open back vowel [ɑ] to begin with and ends with the high, closed vowel [ʊ]. Similarly the diphthong [aɪ] starts with the position of the lowest and most open front vowel [a] and ends in the position of the high front vowel [ɪ] as in the word *high* [haɪ].

## VOWELS ARE TIMED

Each vowel has not only a very definite ~~——~~ d of its own, but each vowel has a time factor in its pronunciation as well. To this we apply the terms *long*, designated in phonetic writing by use of the colon (:) following the written vowel, *half-long* by use of the single dot (.) and *short*, which has no sign other than the symbol itself. Some vowels are long or half-long in accented syllables, depending usually on their position in the word or sentence, and the same vowels may be short in unaccented syllables. The timing of the vowels, it should be noted, has nothing to do with the distinctive character of the sound of the vowel; it has to do only with the length of time the vowel is sounded. But timing of vowels is an important factor in good American speech, for it puts a stamp of emphasis and significance upon the speaker's expression.

While the timing of single vowels does not change their particular character, it has a very strong influence on the diphthong. In the pronunciation of diphthongs the first vowel is quite long but the second should be touched very lightly and dropped. In writing diphthongs phonetically we often put a breve ( ˘ ) over the second vowel to indicate its very short length in comparison with the first vowel.

## TO SUMMARIZE

From the descriptions of all the actions of jaw, tongue and lips that create speech, there are a number of general, but concrete, observations to be made that could be helpful. The shape of the tongue for front and middle vowels is generally convex; for back vowels it is generally concave in front of the PCT. The shape of the lips for front vowels is a horizontal ellipse, corners pulled back; for middle vowels, a small, horizontal oval, corners in; for the three high back vowels, round; for the three low back vowels, a long vertical oval, the corners in, the tongue lying low on the floor of the mouth. (We might say: "Smile on the front vowels, but not on the back vowels.") For the diphthongs, the positions move from the larger opening to the smaller, lips and jaw closing up. In the *Work Book*, Part II, use Exercises I through VII frequently to gain flexibility of tongue, jaw and lips.

It must be remembered that with all these muscle actions in the oral chamber, the voice itself must be sent forward through the chamber with a definite sense of direction, so that a stream of articulated sound will flow through the open gates of the lips. The articulation of vowels is part of resonance. Good American vowels, as orally articulated, are the result of oral resonance with just enough sympathetic nasal resonance added to give them warmth. They must never be choked back in the throat or pinched in the nose. Therefore we shall not put aside practice work in voice, but rather extend the scope of our attention to include the details of fine articualtion, at this point, of particularized vowels.

                ✿    ✿    ✿

"Let me direct you, for the next occasion when you shall bring the vowels *I* and *a* in verbally detached letters into collision, that you do not fill the hiatus with so pronounced a *y*. It is the vulgarization of our tongue which I y-accuse you."

—Dr. Middleton to Clara in THE EGOIST by George Meredith

# GLOSSARY

## VOWELS

| *DESIRABLE* | *UNDESIRABLE* |
|---|---|

1. *PARTICULARIZED VOWELS.* The full gamut of vowel sounds clearly differentiated, the result of flexible actions of the jaw, tongue and lips to form each sound correctly; no substitutions or deviations, yet no pedanticisms or consciously over-careful enunciations.

" 'You shall not press down upon the brow of labor this crown of thorns. . . .' His vowels rang as true as the great orator he was quoting, flinging his unmistak- ̶ ̶ ̶ ̶ ̶ ̶ ̶ ̶ ̶ ̶ ̶ ̶ ̶ ̶ ̶ ̶ ̶ ̶ ̶ ̶ the forced draft of his voice like a banner unfurled and rippling in the wind."

—by a student

1. *INDISTINCT VOWELS.* Slurring, indistinct sounds difficult to identify, the result of little movement of tongue, jaw or lips. The tongue is inflexible; the jaw is rigid; the lips are flabby or tight; sometimes the teeth seem to b e locked together.

"He sounded as though he were clenching a pipe between his teeth. Never once did his lower teeth part from his uppers. He did not speak; he merely rumbled something through the ̶ ̶ ̶ ̶ ̶ ̶ ̶ ̶ ̶ ̶ ̶ ̶ ̶ ̶ ̶ ̶ ̶ well

—by a student

2. *ORALLY RESONATED VOWELS.* Voice is sent forward through individually shaped oral resonance chambers formed by smooth movements of the jaw and tongue. The resulting sound emitted through the sized and shaped doors of the lips is orally resonated voice in articulated vowel sounds.

"Each word, carefully chosen from his superb vocabulary, is as carefully moulded, not merely pronounced, and is smoothly and unobtrusively fitted into the expressive pattern of his resonant voice."

—by a student

2a. *NASALIZED VOWELS.* Sharp and pinched, particularly the front vowels, the result of poor vowel formation in the mouth. The tongue is humped rather high toward the edge of the soft palate for all vowels indiscriminately. The voice is caught and held in a cul-de-sac in the small area beyond the uvula, in the top of the pharynx, or forced up into the narrow nasal passages. From syllable to syllable the tongue moves only with flicks of the tip and blade, the lips but slightly, the jaw hardly at all. At other times a vowel followed by a nasal consonant, *n* especially, often seems to be pulled into the nose with the consonant.

"Her words seemed to jump out of her nose like a swarm of bees and buzz horribly in the ears of the students. When she paused to study her notes, the silence was cool balm on their ears. Then with a sudden lift of her head came another swarm of stinging, humming syllables."

—by a student

2b. *THROATY VOWELS.* Vowel sounds seem to be ground out in a low grumble and rumble, or in a raucous hoarseness that erases the individual character of each vowel. There is often a higher key of nasality heard above the low rumble. Throaty vowels are the result of constriction in the throat and at the back of the mouth; the voice seems to be held down in the throat. Within the oral chamber the tongue lies inflexibly on the floor of the mouth, moving hardly at all, the lips and jaw moving very little more.

"When he spoke, seemingly from his chest, he did not bother to move his jaw or lips and I got the impression he was trying to imitate a ventriloquist."

—by a student

NOTE. Start Assignment II, *Work Book*, pp. ................., at this time. It will be a continually growing list as you listen to the speech of others. Such listening is a most important part of your study.

# Chapter VIII

"The time has come," the Walrus said,
"To talk of many things:
Of me-and thee-and they (or them)
Of busy bees and stings --
And why the terriers chase the cats --
And whether brides have wings."

# The Front Vowels and Diphthongs

A detailed study of all the vowels and diphthongs heard in good American speech is now in order. Using the classification of front, middle and back vowels, we shall consider them in that order. On the following page is a list of the front vowels with IPA symbols, key words and sketches showing the changes in lip shapes and PCT for each vowel. Study the symbols and sketches carefully. Begin at once to associate the written symbols with the sounds. Practice writing them down as you say them, but be sure to check your own sounding of these vowels with your instructor's as he introduces the symbols with the key words to you. If any of the vowels as you sound them differs noticeably from those of your model, do not be content until you know what you do that results in the inaccurate sound; then change it. Experiment with various actions of the tongue, jaw and lips in sounding the vowels until you discover for yourself the correct sound and the action in the making of it. Fix in your concentration the cause and effect relationship of the movements of these organs of articulation with the resulting sounds.

Practice these symbols and sounds over and over. *Write the symbol; sound the vowel.*

CHART OF THE FRONT VOWELS AND DIPHTHONGS IN IPA SYMBOLS WITH KEY WORDS AND DRAWINGS OF THE LIP OPENING FOR EACH VOWEL AND THE CHANGING PLACE OF CONSTRICTION OF THE TONGUE FOR VOWELS AND DIPHTHONGS..

Let us now proceed to a full consideration of each of the ten front vowel sounds.

[i:] as in SHE

*IPA*          *DMS*

[i:]           (ē)—"long e"

*S P E L L I N G S*

she, feel, marine, meat, believe, caffein, paeon, people,
amoeba, quay, key.

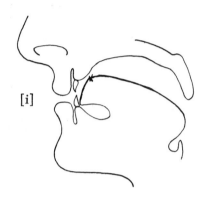

[i]

FIGURE 10

With the PCT high near the upper gum ridge, the corners of the lips pulled back, and the lips open just enough to make a tiny slit between them the sound of the voice sent through this chamber is an unmistakable [i:] as in *she*. This sound is more often long or half-long than short, but it may be cut quite short in words of three or more syllables if the [i] syllable is followed by two unstressed syllables, as in *obesity, eagerness, frequency*. Notice in the list of words above the half-long tim-

ing ~~of the [i] in p~~ ~~ple, amoeba;~~ but in *marine, believe, caffein,* the [i:] is long, falling as it does in the stressed and final syllable. Of all the vowels, [i:] has the smallest lip opening and oral shape, neither of which conditions is calculated to make an easily projected sound in all keys.* However, since it is the most forward vowel in the mouth, it is a good vowel to use in the middle keys for vocal exercising to gain forward projection of the voice through the oral chamber. Recall the use of [mi:] in Exercise VII, Part II of the *Work Book*.

---

*Because of this, composers rarely set this vowel to a high note for singers. The fast, tightly vibrating waves of high pitch within the flat oral chamber of [i:] are uncomfortable for the singer and difficult to sustain.

[ɪ] as in WILL
[ɪɚ] (GA)†, [ɪə] (ES)‡ as in EAR

*IPA*                 *DMS*

1. [ɪ]                 (ĭ)—"short i"
2. [ɪɚ] (GA)
   [ɪə] (ES)

*S P E L L I N G S*

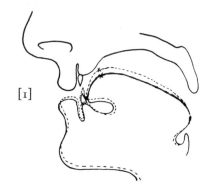

[ɪ]

1. miss, hymn, city, busy, before,   buffet,   mountain,
   scrimmage,   been,   sieve,
   build,, surfeit.
2. ear, here, steer, bombar-
   dier, Hampshire.

FIGURE 11

This is a delicate and very light sound with very little tonal color, with the lightest of vocalized breath sent through a vowel chamber a little larger than the [i:] chamber. From the rather tense [i:] position relax the PCT very slightly and open the jaw a little more to make a trifle larger opening between the lips, making a slightly wider horizontal ellipse. The lightly vocalized breath stream through this aperture will be the fine, delicate sound of [ɪ] heard in these words from the three preceding sentences: this, is, delicate, very, little, with, lightest, position, relax, slightly, opening, between, lips, making, horizontal, ellipse, lightly, will and in.

Too often, however, other vowels are incorrectly substituted for [ɪ]; sometimes the dull, grayish, neutral sound of the indefinite article, "a" beautaful, for example, instead of beautiful; sometimes the pedantic quality of a "short e" in the suffixes "-less" and "-ness," as "neatness" instead ot "neatnis." Or again, in words ending in y the strong [i] is often substituted for the lighter [ɪ], as in "city," seeming to distort the whole word, even to lending a certain quality of infantilism. ("Mom-m-eeee! Johnee took the candee from the babee!") Consider the effect of such distortion on this sentence: "Harry drank a quantity of coffee rapidly after a very tricky examination in history." Not only are these syllables hit hard with the strong, tense, closed [i] but the sound is apt to be drawn out unduly. *In pronouncing the final y, make it light, make it short.*

†General American pronunciation.
‡Eastern Standard pronunciation.

When the vowel sound of [ɪ] is followed by *r* and appears in a stressed syllable at the end of a clause or sentence, it glides into a gentle diphthong [ɪɚ] or [ɪə], with or without a suggestion of an [r] sound, as in these familiar lines:

> "Listen, my children, and you shall h*ear*
> Of the midnight ride of Paul Rev*ere*."

But in this sentence: "You can *hear* the *steers* bellow," the conditions are quite different. The position of the words *hear* and *steers*, as the third and fifth syllables within the seven syllable sentence, times the vowel in each word as a single sound rather than a diphthong.

You will find Exercises V and VI, pp. 105-106, Part II, the *Work Book* helpful in perfecting a fine, delicate [ɪ] vowel.

———————

All together, now! with a great
big cheer!
"Hey, diddle, diddle,"
Said the cat to the fiddle,
"Too late to catch it --
a three-bag hit!"
EE ... Yippeeeeee!

[e] as in DATE
[eɪ] as in DAY

|     | IPA | DMS |
| --- | --- | --- |
| 1. | [e] | (ā)—"long a" |
| 2. | [eɪ̆] |  |

SPELLINGS

1. *a*ging, v*ei*ling, g*au*ging, pl*ay*ing, st*ea*k.
2. th*ey*, p*ai*d, g*ao*l, *a*ge, v*ei*l, pl*ay*.

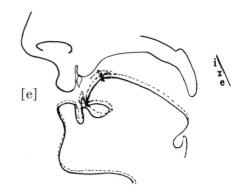

[e]

FIGURE 12

    This strong English vowel is the result of a still more open vowel chamber. The PCT is only half-high in the mouth toward the palate; the lips, still in a horizontal ellipse, well open, but not too far. This sound, too, is heard as a pure vowel in some circumstances and in others as the stronger, longer diphthong [eɪ]. In words of two or more syllables the vowel [e] is usually a single vowel, as in "*way*faring stranger," for example; but when the word containing [e] is a monosyllable, or ends a clause as a final stressed sound, it is then drawn into the diphthong [eɪ]. We tend to close up on a held vowel, the jaw moving up toward a closed position. Pronounce: *aging* and *age, playing* and *play, veiling* and *veil*. Notice how much longer the vowel sound is in the one-syllable word. Again: the vowel is a diphthong in "all work and no *play*" because it is the final syllable in a five-syllable phrase; but in "all *play* and no work" the [e] is a single vowel, for it is now but the second in a five-syllable phrase and in no position of stress. Conceivably, the phrase might be broken into two word groups and "play" prolonged unduly, thus: "all pla-ay - - - and no work." In this case a very special emphasis and implication are laid on it by the speaker.

    Let us look briefly at another circumstance in which the vowel [e] may find itself. Pronounce the words *steak* and *date* again. Notice that, although they are monosyllables, the vowel is nevertheless single, not a diphthong, for the [k] and the [t] break off the flow of the vowel sound neatly and abruptly.

[ɛ] as in ANY
[ɛ:] as in CAREFUL
[ɛɚ] (GA) or [ɛə] (ES) as in CARE

*IPA*           *DMS*
1. [ɛ]         (ĕ)—"short e"
2. [ɛ:]     (â)—"circumflex a"
3. [ɛɚ] (GA)
   [ɛə] (ES)

S P E L L I N G S

1. *any, aesthetic, said, says, ebb, feather, leopard, heifer, friend, bury.*
2. *careful, fairly, prayerful, therefore, bearing.*
~ *~ ~ fair, prayer, where, bear, their.*

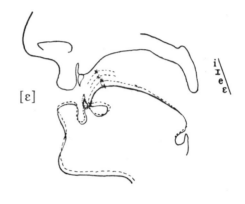

[ɛ]

FIGURE 13

Looking at the chart of Front Vowels (Fig. 10), you will notice that this vowel [ɛ] is rather well down the line representing the changing PCT in its relation to the palate. There is an appreciable opening between the lips as you pronounce [ɛ], but the shape remains a horizontal ellipse. Note, as you pronounce the first group of words above, how short the [ɛ] is regardless of the number of syllables in the word. Now pronounce _____ ___d group in which each [ɛ] is followed by r and an unstressed syllable. In many parts of America ___ _____ to be a change in the vowel itself as a result of a movement of the tip of the tongue upward to pronounce the r. This creates a slightly different vowel from the [ɛ] in the first group of words where r does not appear. This is so general, except in the East, that the dictionaries take note of it with a different diacritical mark, calling it a "circumflex a" (â) instead of a "short e" (ĕ).

While [ɛ:] in the second group of words is but little longer than [ɛ] in the first group, in the third group it is stretched into a diphthong, [ɛɚ] or [ɛə], for the same reason as in the case of the two diphthongs [ɪɚ] or [ɪə] and [eɪ] above. Pronounce: *any prayerful prayer.* Did you notice the short vowel in *any* [ɛnɪ], the longer vowel in *prayerful* [prɛ: fʊl], and the diphthong in *prayer* [prɛɚ] as you spoke the phrase? Remember that if you do sound the (r) following this vowel in such words as *prayer* and *care*, there should be but a suggestion of it. It must be a "monstrous little" [r], as was the voice that Bottom proposed to use in "A Midsummer Night's Dream"; a strong [r] would cover the character of the vowel that precedes it.

[æ] as in HAT

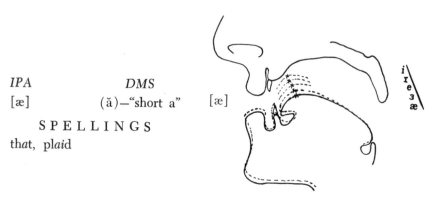

| IPA | DMS | |
|---|---|---|
| [æ] | (ă)—"short a" | [æ] |

S P E L L I N G S

th*a*t,　pl*ai*d

F<small>IGURE</small> 14

This short vowel seems to be almost exclusively an American vowel, as flat and dry as the sun-drenched plateaus of our American West. As is the case with both of the two low front vowels, the PCT is quite low and flat, almost in the floor of the mouth; the lips are distinctly open, the corners pulled back, making a fairly large horizontal ellipse. The voice must be sent forward through the oral resonance chamber thus made for it and "fall forward" out of the opened gates of the lips. "Where did you get that hat?" sang the old-timer, and the vowel [æ] in *that hat* is distinctly larger and flatter than the [ɛ] in *where* and *get*. Too often it hits the ear of the listener with such tightness and sharp nasality as to be a very unpleasant sound.

Moreover, when a word begins with [æ] or [ɛ] both are too frequently initiated with a glottal shock, making a harsh, grating sound, unpleasantly noticeable; rather one should ease into [æ] or [ɛ]. To avoid the danger here of nasalizing these vowels (see GLOSSARY, Chapter 7), concentrate on the fact that all speech sounds are shaped in the oral resonance chamber of the mouth; that in good American speech we do not "intone in the nose ful semely" as did the Nun of Chaucer's Tale. Once more we are made aware of the interrelation of all techniques of voice and speech and their effect, one upon the other.

[a] as in LAUGH
[aɪ] as in NIGHT

*IPA*        *DMS*

1. [a]    (á)—"intermediate a"
2. [aɪ]        (ī)—"long i"

S P E L L I N G S

1. *ask, path, half, laugh, dance.*
2. *night, aisle, aye, height, eye, tie, buy, sky, lye.*

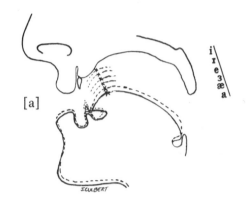

[a]

FIGURE 15

This vowel is the sound in the French word "la." It is softer and more pleasing than the flat [æ]; it is a shorter sound than the broad Italian [ɑ:] as used by the British and cultivated by some Americans, especially in the East. The PCT, still in the front of the mouth, is farthest from the palate for this vowel than for all the front and middle vowels; the lips are rather wide apart, but still in a horizontal ellipse, the corners out, not in. More and more this vowel is being used as a single, pure vowel in good American speech, particularly if in the spelling ...... f.ll....d h., e (*past*). ss (*glass*), f (*after*), th* (*wrath*), nce (*dance*). Many of us would no longer use the [æ] vowel -- -- "I had to *laugh* to see the *calf* go down the *path* in an hour and a *half* and take a *bath* in a minute and a *half.*" One may still hear it, but at one time such a reading was much more common west of the Appalachian Mountains than now. Nor would we read it with the broad [ɑ:] vowel which once was quite common in the East. Rather, you are more likely to hear now a sound about half-way between these two, the low front vowel [a]. The [æ] is still used, however, before *ck* (*lack*), *g* (*bag*), *t* (*mat*), *d* (*had*), *n* (*can*) and *nd* (*land*). Every man wants to be a strong "he-man" [mæn], not a soft [man].

The previous sentence suggests that there is a strong psychological and emotional influence of the vowel sounds in words. The broad [ɑ:]

---

*These four are voiceless consonants.

does not seem to fit the tempo and temperament of Americans. It is a long, almost drawling sound and seems to annoy the average American by its suggestion of affectation, if it is sounded in such common words as *class, path, laugh,* and *half.* On the other hand, the [æ] is too flat with a tendency to be unpleasantly harsh and nasal, while the [a] seems to strike a happy medium with a generally better oral resonance and a nicer distinction in speaking. As we have observed, usage is constantly changing, and we may say that present usage in respect to the use of [æ] and [a] is in a state of flux, not yet definitely standardized. No one will quarrel with you if you use the good American flat [æ] to say: "The *class* [klæs] was dismissed at *half past* [hæf pæst] two," so long as you do not nasalize the [æ]. The use of [a] is growing, however, and you will hear more and more frequently among educated Americans this pronunciation of: "The *class* [klas] was dismissed at *half past* [haf past] two."

The diphthong [aɪ] grows out of this vowel. It is the sound of the personal pronoun *I,* and seems to be a quite different sound from the single vowel [a]. It is a clean, white sound and is made with the wide, quite open lip shape of the vowel [a] to start with, then closes to the [ɪ] position of the jaw, lips and tongue. There are several distortions of this diphthong that are common in certain parts of the country. Let us "take a sounding" of this sentence, for example:

Last *night* the *sky* was so *light* under a *bright,* full moon
*I* could see the *night*ingale in the *cy*press tree.

In the "deep south" one of the dominant characteristics of regional dialect is the substitution of the single front vowel [a] for the diphthong. While it might seem very romantic to hear: "Last [nat] the [ska] was so [lat] under a [brat], full moon [a] could see the [natɪngeɪl] in the [saprɪs] tree," it is still a regional dialect, and as such, not good General American speech. Further west and not so "deep south" is another regional deviation of this sound: the single back vowel [ɑ:] for the diphthong [aɪ]. In southern Illinois and Missouri and the Ozark region you might hear a housewife say: "*Ah* can't stay here talkin'. *Ah* gotta do *mah ahrnin' whahl mah ahrn's* hot." In phonetic script it would be written like this:

[ɑ: gɒtə du mɑ: ɑ:rnin ʍɑ:l mɑ: ɑ:rnz hɒt]

Still another regional distortion of the [aɪ] diphthong is the substitution of the back vowel [ɑ], or even [ɔ] for the front [a], and the high, tight, front [i] for the light [ɪ], making the diphthong dull and dark and very heavy instead of light and bright as [aɪ] should be. The man-on-the-street in New York City would probably read the romantic sentence above like this: "Last [nait] the [skai] was so [lait] under a [brait] full moon [ai] could see the [naitɪngeɪl] in the [saiprɪs] tree." This sound is very unattractive. It is mouthed and covered and certainly robs the sentence of any romantic quality. In the region of New York City, the diphthong ranges from [ɑɪ] to an even darker substitution of a nasalized, painful [ɔ̃i].* This is dialect of a particularly uncultured quality and offends a sensitive ear.

If you are in the habit of sounding [aɪ] incorrectly, then turn to Exercise IX, p. 110., Part II of the *Work Book*. Follow the directions and notes carefully and work with the exercise repeatedly until you have corrected the diphthong.

## TO SUMMARIZE

We would remind you on____   ___ that each of the six front vowels is created by particular muscle movements of the ____  ___ jaw and lips. Each is a combination of a particular amount of jaw and lip openin_, and a particular amount of tongue constriction. From high to low each vowel has a slightly larger opening than the preceding, and the PCT is a little farther back. Remember, too, that the shape of the tongue for all front vowels is a gentle convex curve.

Having studied the Front Vowels, now do Assignment IV, Part II, _ ¹⁰² the *Work Book*.

*"Hey diddle diddle,*
*Said the cat to the fiddle,*
*"See the pretty lass*
*Lying on the grass.*
*O what a pretty lass,*
*Pretty lass, pretty lass;*
*O what a pretty lass*
*Is lying on the grass!"*

---

*IPA symbol for a nasalized vowel is a wave [~] over it, thus: [ɔ̃].

# PRONUNCIATIONS

## FRONT VOWELS

NOTE. Practice reading aloud the sentences below in both columns. Deliberately sound the vowels as indicated by the IPA symbols, whether you know them to be correct or not. Listen with concentration to each vowel you make and fix in your memory the difference between the desirable and undesirable sounds.

### DESIRABLE

1. [i:]—*she* [ʃi:]; long.
   [i.]—*people* [pi.pl]; half-long.
   [i]—*leniency* [linɪənsɪ]; short.
   A strong vowel; PCT high, front; lips open a tiny slit.

   *She* [ʃi:] *belongs to the people* [pi.pl] *and in the people* [pi.pl] *there is no leniency* [linɪənsɪ].

### UNDESIRABLE

1a. [i]—cut short in monosyllables, especially at end of phrases.

   "*He joined the navy to see* [si] *the world;*
   *And what did he see* [i si]? *He* [hi] *saw the sea* [si]."

1b. [ɪi:]—an on-glide; the sound of the vowel starts while the tongue is still moving into position.

   *Give it to me* [mɪi].

1c. [iɪ]—an off-glide to [ɪ]; position of articulators taken for [i:]; is not held, but slides off to [ɪ].

   *You are now free* [friɪ].

2a. [ɪ]—*city* [sɪtɪ]; very short, very light. Relax both the PCT and the lips slightly from the above position.

   *The city* [sɪtɪ] *slicker* [slɪk-] *and the country* [-trɪ] *bumpkin* [-kɪn] *were obviously* [ɒbvɪəslɪ] *enjoying* [-ɪŋ] *themselves.*

2. Substitutions for [ɪ]:
   [ə]—result of very lazy tongue action.

   *Do you believe* [bəli:v] *in spirits* [spərəts]?

   —[ɛ]—pedantic; overdone, too precise; somewhat affected.

   "*Look Children* [-drɛn]," *she said,* "*The trees are all leafless* [liflɛs], *and now they have the neatness* [nitnɛs] *of sheer lace against the horizon. What loveliness!* [lʌvlɪnɛs].

2b. [ɪə]—*here* [hɪə]; an off-glide into the middle, neutral vowel, making a diphthong. In the spelling an *r* always follows the vowel; the vowel *may* be a substitute for the [r], especially in Eastern Standard speech.

*With such dreary** [drɪrɪ] *news, a mere* [mɪə] *whisper is enough to sear* [sɪə] *my ears* [ɪəz].

2c. [ɪɚ]—*here* [hɪɚ]; good General American; an off-glide from the diphthong to a very slight touch of the [r].

*The Wierd* [wɪɚd] *Sisters were the queerest* [kʍɪrɪst]* *creatures of Shakespeare's* [-pɪɚz]

—[i]—too heavy in final *y* syllables.

*We have only* [onli] *lately* [letli] *realized that we are well into the second fifty* [fɪfti] *years of the century* [sɛntʃuri].

3a. [e]—*date* [det], *rake* [rek]; vowel cut short by the stop consonants [t] and [k]. PCT still farther from the palate; wider ellipse of the lip opening.

*It is too late* [let] *now to rake* ˌ before *dark.*

3a. [ẽ]†—nasalized; no jaw movement, practically no opening between the lips; the least possible tongue movement in the mouth. The sound itself is pulled up into the nasal chamber and emanates, seemingly, from the nostrils.
*He came* ˌ the track *at a great* [grẽt] *pace* [pẽɪs].

3b. [eɪ]—*day* [deɪ]; the held first vowel glides into [ɪ], becoming a diphthong by a slight upward movement of the jaw. This is a very strong sound.
*Let's spend the day* [deɪ] *on the bay* [beɪ].

3b. [ẽɪə]; very long, drawled, becoming a triphthong; generally nazalized as well; lazy speech, and whining.

*The color drained* [drẽɪənd] *from her face* [fẽɪəs] *when the pain* [pẽɪən] *came* [keɪəm], *and she was ghostly pale* [pẽɪəl].

---

*No diphthong when [r] initiates a following syllable.
†This mark ( ˜ ) over an IPA symbol indicates a nasalized vowel.

4a. [ɛ]—*met* [mɛt]; short and light if there is no *r* in the spelling.

*Bess* [bɛs] *left* [lɛft] *a dreadful* [drɛdful] *mess* [mɛs] *at the head* [hɛd] *of the steps* [stɛps].

4b. [ɛ:]—*careful* [kɛ:ful]; longer and stronger than [ɛ]; slightly different character of sound when followed by [r] plus a weak syllable.

*Thereafter* [ðɛ:raftɚ] *he drove more carefully* [kɛ:fulɪ].

4c. [ɛɚ] or [ɛə] — *fair* [fɛɚ]; a smooth, gliding diphthong in a monosyllable. The [r] must never be sounded strongly, if at all.

*She stared* [stɛɚd] *at the fair-haired* [fɛ:hɛɚd] *girl at the foot of the* [stɛɚz].

4a. [ɛ̃]*—nasalized, pinched whine, most unpleasant; often drawled into a diphthong.

*Freddie* [frɛ̃dɪ], *don't set* [sɛ̃t] *the kettle* [kɛ̃tl] *on the bed* [bɛ̃d].

4b. [ɛ̃r]†—nasalized vowel followed by strongly inverted [r] destroys the character of this vowel altogether.

*Carol* [kɛ̃rəl], *are you up there* [ðɛ̃r]? *Did you take that pair* [pɛ̃r] *of chairs* [tʃɛ̃rz] *upstairs* [ʌpstɛ̃rz]?

4c. Substitutions for [ɛ] in diphthong [ɛɚ]:

—[æ]; the tongue is too low in the mouth, making a flat, uninteresting sound of the first vowel.

*Warning: Do not feed the brown bears* [bæɚz]. *Beware* [-wæɚ] *those bears* [bæɚz].

—[eɪ]—another regionalism, often heard in the Middle West.

*Can you unscramble eggs* [eïgz]?

—[ɪ]—often careless speech; sometimes regional dialect; or possibly a foreignism.

(a) *He didn't exactly* [ɪgzæklɪ] *get* [gɪt] *an education* [ɪdʒɪkeʃən].

(b) *How many* [mɪnɪ] *men* [mɪn] *were in the tent* [tɪnt]?

(c) *Have you ever* [ɪvɚ] *felt* [fɪlt] *the edge* [ɪdʒ] *of a feather* [fɪðɚ]?

---

*This mark ( ˜ ) over an IPA symbol indicates a nasalized vowel.
†To indicate an inversion with IPA symbols put a dot (.) below the symbol, thus: [r̩], (l̩), [ɔ̩].

5. [æ]–*flat, land* [flæt, lænd]; a very *flat,* strong sound; always spelled with an *a.*

*The Owl and the Pussycat* [-kæt], *hand* [hænd] *in hand* [hænd] *on the edge of the sand* [sænd], *danced* [dænst]* *by the light of the moon.*

5a. [æ̃] nasalized. Of all the vowels the most often pinched and nazalized; m o s t unpleasant. Sometimes also drawled into a pinched diphthong.

*Is Dandy* [dæ̃ndɪ] *Andy* [æ̃ndɪ] *taking you to the dance* [dæ̃əns]?

5b. Substitutions for [æ]:
—[ɛ]; foreignism or illiterate speech.
*That* [ðɛt] *cab* [kɛb] *is an old rattle-trap* [rɛtl trɛp].

—[a], and often a nasalized [ã] if followed by a nasal consonant; the vowel is pulled into the nose, with the result of a heady hum instead of a clear vowel.

ᵀᴸ ᵇ~~ᵈᵘ [hãndɪ] *man* [mãn] *drank* ⌊drãŋk⌋ ᵃᵘ ᵗⁿᵉ ᵛ~~~~ᵧ [brãndɪ].

6a. [a]–*raft* [raft], *class* [klas], *path* [paθ]; a softer, more pleasant sound than the [æ] above; most open of the front vowels; always spelled with an *a.*

*From the path* [paθ] *below* ᵘᵘᵘᵍᵐᵛ. [waftɪd] *through the open windows to the distraction of the class* [klas] *within.*

6a. [ã] nasalized; especially if followed by a nasal consonant, as in the cases above. [a] loses its character completely when nasalized, becoming an indefinite "nosey" sound and giving the impression of affectation.

a. *He nunuies* [~~~~~] ᵘ ᶠ~~~ [fãnsɪ] *brand* [brãnd] *of candy* [kãndɪ].

b. *"Dance* [dãns], *dance, dance all night."*

6b. [aɪ]–*pie* [paɪ]; open, low front vowel, gliding into the closed, high front vowel [ɪ] making the diphthong.

6b. [ãɪ] nasalized and drawled, especially when followed by a nasal consonant; very unpleasant.

*Dance is one of those words that is changing in pronunciation. You will hear it both as [dænst] and [danst] from educated people. This writer believes it is being pronounced more and more often as [danst].

*This is a bright* [braɪt] *sound, a white* [ʍaɪt] *sound, made with lips wide* [waɪd] *open.*

*In my* [mãɪ] *mind* [mãɪnd] *a decidedly* [dɪsãɪdɪdlɪ] *different line* [lãɪn] *of action might* [mãɪt] *be tried* [trãɪd].

6c. Substitutions for [aɪ]:

—[ɑɪ]—low back vowel; makes the diphthong a "dull gray" rather than a "bright white" tone.

*When the dyke* [dɑɪk] *went, there was a wild* [wɑɪld] *scramble for higher* [hɑɪɚ] *and drier* [drɑɪɚ] *ground.*

—[ɔɪ]—dark, covered, mouthed, unclear; an especially distorted substitution; seems to be swallowed; very unpleasant.

*I'll* [ɔɪl] *have a slice* [slɔɪs] *of that fine* [fɔɪn] *pie* [pɔɪ].

—[ai:]—off-glide into a long tense [i:] for the second vowel; an infantilism; affected good cheer. *Goodbye* [-bai:]; *have a wonderful time* [tai:m]; *be sure to write* [rai:t].

—[a]—the pure low front vowel for the diphthong, eliminating the off-glide; characteristic of southern dialect.

*"My* [ma] *time* [tam] *is your time"* [tam].

—[ɑ]—the single, low, back vowel for the diphthong; no off-glide; southern central regional dialect, difficult to understand b e c a u s e syllables are so mouthed.

*"Strike* [strɑ:k] *while* [ʍɑ:l] *the iron's* [ɑ:rnz] *hot,"* I [ɑ:] *always say.*

NOTE. Now you should begin to keep a list of those vowels you habitually mispronounce. Assignment V, Part II, p. 105, the *Work Book*, is, therefore, a continuing assignment for the rest of your study.

# Chapter IX

"H'm to talk -- to talk --," the Walrus mused,
"In less than thirty words --
Of monkeys cussing at circus pups,
Of fluttering, flirting birds."

"No cussing," said the Carpenter,
"Miss Muffets eating her curds."

## The Middle Vowels

As their name implies, the middle vowels are made with the PCT in the middle of the tongue and the mouth open half-way. One might think these to be the easiest vowels to pronounce correctly. They are, but precisely because they are in the middle, they are in danger of being indistinct from sheer laziness of tongue and jaw.

Referring to the key words for each front vowel on the chart, Figure 9, (Chapter 8) you will remember that they are part of a sentence which continues with the key words of the three middle vowels. The three vowels of the last two words of that sentence are to be our consideration in this chapter.

Study the chart of the middle vowels, FIGURE 16. Note that the line of front vowels with key words is included in order to show the relationship of the middle vowels to them. The back vowels will be placed along the right oblique line of the PCT in the next chapter. Notice the oval shape of the lips for these middle vowels and the low position of the mildly convex curve of the tongue.

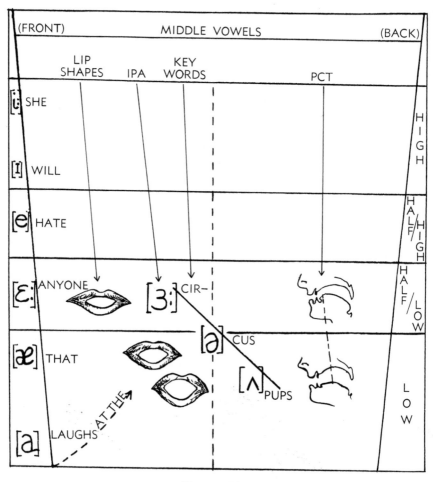

FIGURE 16

THE MIDDLE VOWELS IN IPA SYMBOLS WITH DAWINGS OF
LIP SHAPES AND PCT.

[ɝ] (GA) or [ɜ:] (ES) as in *CIRCUS*

| IPA | DMS |
|---|---|
| [ɝ] (GA) | (û),(ĕ) |
| [ɜ:] (ES) | |

S P E L L I N G S
b*ir*d, f*ur*, p*er*t, m*yr*tle, w*or*d,
c*our*tesy, *ear*nest, amat*eur*.

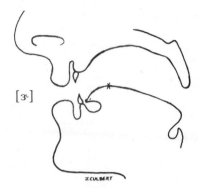

[ɝ]

J.CULBERT

FIGURE 17

This is another of those vowels which, in the spelling, is always followed by *r*. Across the country one may hear many variations in the pronunciation ———— ———— —————— the furry worm." ranging from a colorless vowel without the shadow of an *r* to a "vowel-less souna of the *r* itself burring in one's ears. What is the right of it? Shall we follow the adage "When in Rome, do as the Romans do"? Then we would drop the *r* in New England, but in Boston put it on again where it never was (the idear!); drop it in New York and below the Mason-Dixon Line, where we would never find it again. In the Midwest we would need it, much or little, depending on whether we were down on the farm in Indiana, Illinois, Kansas or Missouri, where we would ———— ——— [r] we could churn up.

Now, however, through the great reaches of radio and ————— ————— and the influence of the good speech of the Edward R. Murrows, the Lowell Thomases, the John Dalys, the Richard Evanses, and many others, a general American standard in respect to the *r* is becoming established. We are finding a happy medium between the extremes of "*r*-less vowels and vowel-less *r*'s." The answer to the question, then, is to pronounce [ɝ:] as a long pure vowel (never a diphthong) with just a suggestion of *r* in the sound. To make [ɝ:] raise the tongue half-way in the mouth toward the palate. The tongue is in a gentle convex curve from tip to back with very little constriction. Take care that the tip of the tongue does not turn up to meet the upper gum ridge, for then the sound of the vowel is caught in a pocket created by that inverted tongue tip; the vowel loses its character and may all but disappear.

[ə] as in CIRCUS

*IPA*              *DMS*

1. [ə]    (ȧ),(ă),*(ĕ),*(ĭ),*
                  (ŏ),*(ŭ)

2. [ɝ]    (ē̃)

S P E L L I N G S

1. circus, about, surgeon, fur-
   ious, waistcoat, tortoise,
   analysis, atom, possible,
   villain, nation, quiet, the
   conform.
2. sister, harbor, martyr, particular.

[ə]

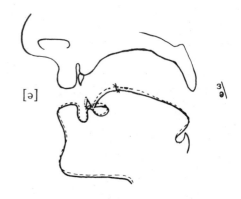

FIGURE 18

This is the most colorless, neutral and relaxed of all the vowels. It is, in fact, a sound so elusive and yet so ubiquitous that DMS attempts to capture it by using six different symbols with all the five vowel letters in the alphabet. This weak, gray sound never occurs in the strong syllable of a word, but only in unstressed syllables. Obviously, [ə] is the least definite of all the vowels shaping it with boundaries indicated but not determined, like a fuzzy image on a television screen. It is the easiest vowel to make, and the most often heard, for the very little activity of the articulators in making it encourages us to level all vowels to it. The tongue lies relaxed, the lips are but little more open than for the [ɜ] above it, and there is hardly more than a puff of voice. These middle vowels are decidedly unmusical, having very little tonal quality.

Notice that we have the two IPA symbols, one with and one without an [r]. In the second group of words note that an r follows the vowel. It is generally the speaking habit of educated Americans to give a slight [r] sound in such words as *sister, harbor, martyr, particular,* where r ends the last syllable. The phonetic symbol for this sound is [ɝ], a modification of [ə]. Pronounce the second group of words above. Do you hear only the neutral [ə]? or do you hear [ɝ]? If the latter, be careful to make only the whisper of an r trailing after the [ə] and write it [ɝ].

---

*Concerning the DMS symbol the italic ĭ, DMS, indicates a variation, in good usage, from [ɪ] to [ə]. This is equally true of (ă) which varies from [æ] to [ə], of (ĕ) which varies from [ɛ] to [ə], and of (ŏ) which varies from [ɒ] to [ə].

[ʌ] as in PUPS

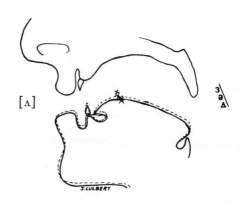

*IPA*          *DMS*

[ʌ]    (ŭ), (ȯ)—"short u"

S P E L L I N G S

p*u*p, c*o*me, d*oe*s, c*ou*ple, fl*oo*d

FIGURE 19

This vowel is much stronger than the [ə] and is generally found in ~~stressed syllables, rarely in an unstressed syllable~~. On the vowel chart (Figure 16) you will notice that the PCT is very low, near the position for the back vowels; the mouth is open appreciably, giving to the [ʌ] more tonal resonance than the neutral vowel above it, though the two are often very close in sound. It is the vowel sound in such common words as *come, shun, such, dull, humdrum* and *dozens* of *others.* You will hear it sometimes in the prepositions *up, of* and *from* when they fall in positions of special emphasis.

At this point it is appropriate to note that prepositions which are ordinarily weak words in a sentence may have considerable variety in the strength of the vowel sound. Among these positions the vowel in *from*, for instance, runs the gamut from a strong [ʌ] through the [ə] to its disappearance altogether, as in these phrases:

    1. Going to and *from*—[frʌm]
    2. Candy *from* the baby—[frəm]
    3. *From* all we can tell—[frm]

In fact all prepositions undergo similar variability according to their relative emphasis in phrases and sentences. Conjunctions are also subject to variability of strong vowels and weak vowels according to their varying emphasis values. *But* is [bʌt] or [bət]; *and* ranges in strength from [ænd] to [ənd] to [nd] to [n]. It is important to have developed an acute ear for these degrees of change.

## TO SUMMARIZE

We must be very particular in making the three middle vowels to guard against the constant inclination to indolence of the articulators and the tendency, consequently, to level all vowels to the [ə], the weakest and least characterful of all. We should remember that the [ɜ] is always followed by an r in the spelling, and in good General American speech there is a slight sound of [r] in the vowel itself, but only slight. This vowel is nearest the [ɛ] front vowel in position, which is also influenced frequently by a following r. The vowel [ʌ], on the other hand, is nearest the back vowel [ɒ], which is sometimes incorrectly, substituted for the [ʌ] by overly pedantic or emphatic speakers. As with all vowels, each middle vowel is a specific sound in itself, like no other.

Do Assignment VI at this point; p. 106, Part II, the *Work Book*.

✻     ✻     ✻

"And it is so plain to me that eloquence, like swimming, is an art which all men might learn, though so few do."

—Ralph Waldo Emerson

"Such a voice, such diction and such a gift for maintaining the melody of Shakespeare's verse even while keeping it edged from speech to speech with dramatic significance, is a new experience. . . . He is no mere reciter of what he has to say. . . . He turns the searchlight of his thinking and his feeling on sentence after sentence that gains a new force and a new meaning because of what he finds to reveal."

—John Mason Brown, speaking of GIELGUD'S HAMLET

# PRONUNCIATIONS

## MIDDLE VOWELS

NOTE: Practice reading aloud the sentences below in both columns. Deliberately sound the vowels as indicated by the IPA symbols, whether you know them to be correct sounds or not. Listen with concentration to each vowel you make and fix in your memory the difference between the desirable and undesirable sounds.

### DESIRABLE

1a. [ɜ:] (ES)—*curd* [kɜ:d], *yearn,* [jɜ:n], *word* [wɜ:d]. *irk* [ɜ:k]; tip of tongue behind lower front teeth; PCT relaxed slightly in the middle of the mouth.

*Sh̲ ̲h̲e̲a̲r̲d̲ [hɜ:d] every word* [wɜ:d] *through the thin walls, and it irked* [ɜ:kt] *her* [hɜ:] *not to be able to reply at once.*

1b. [ɝ] (GA)—(Same key words as above.) After the vowel is made in the mouth, the blade of the tongue rises very slightly adding a suggestion of the [r] sound. ̲ ̲ ̲ ̲American speech and more widespread over the country than Eastern Standard.

*She heard* [hɝd] *every word* [wɝd] *through the thin walls, and it irked* [ɝkt] *her* [hɝ] *not to be able to reply.*

### UNDESIRABLE

1a. [ɜɪ]; diphthongized. Too flat and drawn out; sounds affected.

*Word* [wɜɪd] *reached us of the death of Major Byrd* [bɜɪd] *on Thursday* [θɜɪzdɪ].

1b. [ɝ] strong, inverted [ɽ] sound covering the vowel. Tip of tongue curled back and up to palate, creating a "pocketed," strong *r*. Midwestern regionalism.

*We call the helicopter* [ ̲ ̲ ̲ ̲ ̲ ̲ ̲. whirly* [ʍɝlɪ] *bird* [bɝd].

1c. *Substitution* for [ɜ]: —[ɔɪ] Diphthong substituted in various degrees of broadness. It is the New York City's taxicab driver's sharp, hard, back vowel.

*That's the first* [fɔɪst] *house between Third* [θɔɪd] *Avenue and Irving* [ɔɪvɪŋ] *Place, Ma'am.*

2a. [ə]—*above* [əbʌv]; the sound of least character, colorless and neutral; always in a weak, unstressed syllable. Very relaxed tongue; hardly a n y PCT. Sounded more often than any other vowel.

"*Above* [əbʌv] *and* [ənd] *beyond the* [ðə] *call of* [əv] *duty.*"

2a. Substitution: A strong vowel substituted for [ə] in final or next to final syllables ending in *r*.

*The monitor* [mɒnɪtɔɚ] *was told to be particularly* [pətɪkjʊlɑ˞:lɪ] *alert in this class.*

2b. [ɚ] — *another* [ənʌðɚ]; final syllables of -*er* may have a very light suggestion of [r]. The tongue moves very slightly, the blade rising a trifle.

*What a bother* [-ðɚ] *to wear rubbers* [-bɚz] *when the weather* [-ðɚ] *is colder* [-dɚ].

2b. [ɝ] — *mother* [mʌðɝ] v e r y strong [r] sound in final *er* syllables; inverted tongue "pockets" the vowel sound unpleasantly.

*Fathers* [-ðɝz], *mothers* [-ðɝz], *sisters* [-tɝz], *brothers* [-ðɝz] *followed the Piper* [-pɝ] *for their lives.*

3. [ʌ] — *cup* [kʌp]: lower and darker than above; almost a back vowel; usually in a stressed syllable.

"*My cup* [kʌp] *runneth* [rʌnɪθ] *over.*"

3. Substitution for [ʌ]:—[ɒ] *butter* [bɒtɚ]: pedantic, affected.

*They have come* [kɒm] *to see that justice* [dʒɒstɪs] *is done* [dɒn].

NOTE. Now begin Assignment VII, p. 107, Part II, the *Work Book*.

\*    \*    \*

"She spoke with brisk, jerky motions of the lower jaw and quick, emphatic nods. She used no dialect, but enunciated clearly and with precision, stressing the consonants. Vowel sounds, however, she exaggerated so much that she said, for instance, 'botter' for 'butter'— or even 'batter'! Her little dog she called 'Babby' insteady of 'Bobby.' She would say to a pupil: 'Don't be so stu-upid, child,' and give two quick knocks on the table with her knuckle. It was very impressive—no doubt whatever about that."

—of Fraulein Weichbrodt in BUDDENBROOKS by Thomas Mann

# Chapter X

*"The time is now," the Walrus said,*
*"To talk of the dark, dark sounds,*
*The vowels of ah and awe*
*          and oh and oo,*
*The long vowels and the round;*
*and why so often mispronounced--*
*And whether spooks abound.*

# The Back Vowels and Diphthongs

The tonal color and timing of the back vowels is decidedly different from the tonal color and timing of the front and middle vowels. The back vowels have considerably more resonance, are rounder and darker and take longer to sound than do the front vowels. The poets appreciate this difference not only for the music of expression, but for the meaningfulness of what they are saying, as well.

Because it is such a short step from [ʌ], the lowest and farthest back of the middle vowels, to the lowest and farthest front of the back vowels, we shall consider these vowels in succession from low to high. The sentence of key words for the back vowels, therefore, reads up the line of the chart, Figure 20.

| DIPHTHONGS | | BACK VOWELS | | |
|---|---|---|---|---|
| PCT | IPA | PCT | LIP SHAPES | IPA |
| | YOUR [ʊə] | | CANOE [u:] | HIGH |
| | | | THE TOOK [ʊ] | |
| | SO [ɒʊ] | THE CHANGING PCT | JOE SO BOAT [o] | HALF/HIGH |
| | OIL [ɔɪ] OAR [ɔə] | | BROAD [ɔ:] | HALF/LOW |
| | OWL [ɑʊ] | | WANTED THE [ɒ] | LOW |
| | | | CARL [ɑ:] | |

FIGURE 20

CHART OF THE BACK VOWELS AND DIPHTHONGS IN IPA SYMBOLS WITH KEY WORDS AND DRAWINGS OF THE LIP OPENINGS FOR EACH VOWEL AND THE CHANGING PLACE OF CONSTRICTION OF THE TONGUE FOR VOWELS AND DIPTHONGS.

Study the sounds and symbols with concentration. Note the PCT* and the shape of the lips for each back vowel; form them and sound them carefully. Fix the sounds in your ears, the shapes in your mind, and write the symbol for each vowel as you sound it. Do this many times until the sound and the symbol are automatically synonymous. One of the first observations to make is that when we sound the back vowels in succession from low to high, the shape of the lips changes from vertically elliptical to rounded.

*Referring, of course, to the Place of Constriction of the Tongue in its relation to the palate.

# THE VERTICALLY ELLIPTICAL VOWELS

[ɑ:] as in FATHER
[aŭ] as in OUT

| | IPA | DMS |
|---|---|---|
| 1. | [ɑ:] | ä |
| 2. | [ɑ˞] | (är) |
| 3. | [aŭ] | (ou) |

SPELLINGS

1. c*a*lm, f*a*ther.
2. C*a*rl, he*a*rth, s*er*geant, mem*oi*r.
3. n*ow*, *ou*t, b*ough*, sau*er*kr*au*t.

[ɑ:]

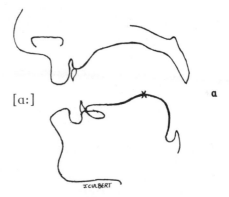

ɑ

J. CULBERT

FIGURE 21

This is the freest, most open of all the vowels. Drop the jaw far down and let the tongue lie on the floor of the mouth with a very slight constriction back of the middle. Be very sure that the tongue is *not* pulled back and humped up high, blocking the entrance into the oral chamber. Now send voice through this wide open chamber and you will sound the [ɑ:] vowel, the most resonant of all the vowels. Notice in the second group of words above that *r* follow— [ɔ] —— pronounce them, supply a very small suggestion of the *r*, if any: *Carl* [kɑ˞l], *heart* [hɑ˞t], etc.

This free, open vowel is the first element of the most frequently used of all the dipthongs, [aʊ], found in so many common words, as in *downtown* and *round about*. In spite of the fact that the stronger sound [ɑ:] is so free and open, one often hears substitutions of the low front [a], and even of the very flat [æ], accompanied usually by unpleasant nasalization, especially if the dipthong is followed by *n;* [daʊntaʊn] becomes [dãʊntãʊn] or even [dæ̃ʊntæ̃ʊn]. As we know, when this occurs the jaw, tongue and lips are forming a different vowel chamber from the one called for and, in addition, the voice is sent up into the nose instead of forward through the mouth. It is as simple as that. But to change that habit, while simple enough in essence, calls for a great many consciously repeated performances of opening the jaw wide and keeping the tongue low, thus freeing the entrance into the oral chamber and allowing the voice to move forward through the mouth for good oral resonance.

If this dipthong is one of your errors in speech turn to Exercise X, p. 144, Part II, the *Work Book*. Carefully following the directions and notes, work on this sound until you have corrected it.

[ɒ] as in WANTS

*IPA*                *DMS*
[ɒ]              (ŏ)—"short o"

S P E L L I N G S
not, song, want, Lawrence, laurel.

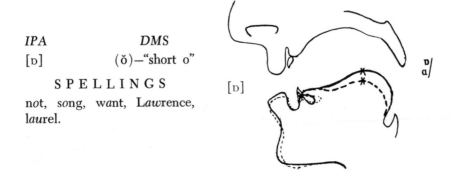

FIGURE 22

This vowel is a short, sharp sound when followed by [t], as in *not*, or by one of the other stop consonants; a little longer and not so sharp when followed by one of the continuant consonants. Many people interchange the two low back vowels, [ɑ] and [ɒ], making little, if any, distinction between them. The [ɑ:] in *father* [fɑ:ðɚ] would then have the slightly darker sound of [ɒ] in *watch* [wɒtʃ], or *watch* the more open vowel in *father*. Others substitute the much darker vowel of the "open o," [ɔ], especially if the back nasal consonant [ŋ] follows the vowel as in *song*, *long*, etc. Actually [ɒ] lies between [ɑ] and [ɔ]. It is nearer [ɑ], however, and the substitution of [ɑ] for [ɒ] does not offend the ears as the darker [ɔ] substitution frequently does.

[ɔ:] as in BROAD
[ɔɪ] as in VOICE
[ɔɚ] or [ɔə] as in POUR

| IPA | DMS |
|---|---|
| 1. [ɔ:] | (ô), "circum-flex o" (aw) |
| 2. [ɔɪ] | (oi) |
| 3. [ɔɚ] | (ör)* |
| [ɔə] | |

S P E L L I N G S

1. call, fork, sauce, fought, George, broad, law.
2. joy, voice.
3. pour, core, boar, Boer, ᵈᵒᵒʳ

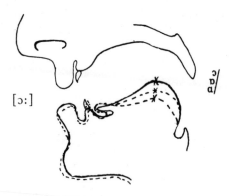

[ɔ:]

FIGURE ₂₀

This vowel is sometimes called the "open o," for it is distinctly a more open sound than [o] and is in the low, back vowel group. In pronouncing it give the lips a vertical-oval shape rather than a round shape. With the tip of the tongue against the lower gum ridge, the PCT is a decided hump just back of the middle of the tongue. In reading up the line of back vowels we begin with the large oval shape to produce [ɑ:], and gradually "close the mouth" to make each higher vowel in succession. At the same time we pull the tongue back a little more for each vowel, making a little higher hump each time.

Again you must remember to send the voice forward through the oral chamber for good vowel clarity and particularity. It is especially important to do so for the [ɔ:] vowel, which is the transition vowel between the round, high back vowels and the lower, open, oval back vowels. Too often in sounding the [ɔ:] the voice is held back and down in the throat with the lips round as for [o], preventing a clear articulation. The effect is unpleasant, the vowel indistinct and almost toneless. If it is necessary for you to correct this vowel, use Exercise XI, p. 150, Part II, *The Work Book*. Carefully follow the directions and notes.

*As this DMS (ör) suggests, *for* and *four* are often pronounced with the pure [o], especially if the *r* initiates another syllable, as in *oral*. We believe, however, that the open [ɔ] is in more general usage in such words.

There are two diphthongs based on this vowel: [ɔɪ], as in *voice*, and [ɔɚ] or [ɔə], as in *pour*. To make [ɔɪ] the PCT glides forward from [ɔ] to the position for the front vowel [ɪ], and the lips stretch into the long, narrow, horizontal ellipse. To make [ɔə] the PCT glides into the middle of the tongue and the lips spread slightly at the corners to a horizontal oval. In making a diphthong the movement from one vowel to the other must be so swift, so smooth and so finely timed, that the resulting sound appears almost as a single vowel. Obviously, this calls for fine flexibility of the articulators. To this end you should be practicing the exercises in Part II of *The Work Book* assiduously.

Notice the timing of the [ɔ:] in *pour* in this dialogue:

> Mother: Who wants to *pour* the lemonade?
>
> Small daughter: Oh, please, may I *pour*?
>
> Mother: Yes, dear, but be careful not to *pour* it too fast.

In these three sentences there are three different degrees of timing of the [ɔ] in *pour*. In the first, it is a long, pure vowel, [ɔ:]; in the second, as a monosyllable at the end of a sentence, it is distinctly a diphthong, [ɔɚ] or [ɔə]; in the third it is a half-long vowel with the [r] elided into the next vowel and initiating a new syllable, so that "pour it" becomes [pɔ rɪt].

## THE ROUND BACK VOWELS

For the three low back vowels, as we have seen, the lips form vertical ovals. But the three high back vowels are made with the lips rounded in three differently sized circles. Moving up the line from [ɔ:] to [o] (Figure 20), the lips are pursed forward slightly into a fairly large circle which becomes smaller and smaller as we pronounce the next two vowels above it. The lips must never be flattened in pronouncing any of the three high back vowels.

*Oh, look at this gooky goo.*

[o] as in HOTEL
[oʊ] as in JOE

*IPA*　　　*DMS*
1. [o]　　　(ō)—"long o"
2. [oʊ]

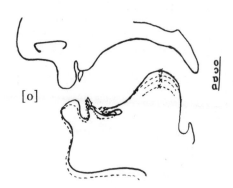

[o]

SPELLINGS

1. hotel, vaudeville, boat.
2. beau, Joe, row, oh, though.

FIGURE 24

In the sentence of key back vowels, *Carl wanted the broad boat, so Joe took the canoe,* the word *boat* lies in the middle and has very little emphasis; *boat* is, then, a comparatively weak syllable and therefore takes the short, single vowel [o]. Furthermore, the [o] in *boat* is followed by a light stop consonant, which cuts short the vowel stream of sound. The same circumstances influence this vowel as do the front vowel [e] in respect to timing; *lateness* [let-] *of the day* [dei], for example. However, when the [o] sound occurs _____ _____ _____ _____ in a strong position, as in the word *Joe* in the key sentence (Figure 20) the [o] is lengthened perceptibly and followed by an off glide into [ʊ] making the diphthong [oʊ]. For another example—*Please go; and go quickly.*—the word *go* is first a diphthong [oʊ] because of its stress in the sentence, while the second *go* is a single vowel [o] because of its lack of stress, *quickly* being the word of emphasis in the second clause.

Sometimes we hear a flattening of the [o] because the lips are not sufficiently rounded. The result is an "on-glide" diphthong, [εo], a sound not recognized nor accepted in good American speech. The general effect is one of bored laziness and almost comic affectation and superciliousness. Anyone who cares about the distinction of his speech will not allow his muscles of articulation to become lazy and slack.

[ʊ] as in TOOK
[ʊɚ] (GA) or [ʊə] (ES) as in YOUR

IPA                DMS
1. [ʊ]           (ŭ), (o̧), (oŏ)
2. [ʊɚ] (GA)     (oŏr)
   [ʊə] (ES)

SPELLINGS

1. put, good, should, wolf.
2. poor, your, allure.

[ʊ]

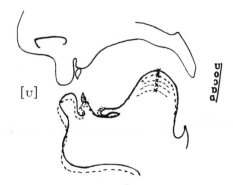

FIGURE 25

This vowel lacks tonal color. The lips are a little more tightly rounded than for the more open, round [o], but they are more relaxed than when making the tensely rounded, high back vowel [u:]. [ʊ] bears the same relationship to [u] as [ɪ] to [i] and appears at the same level on the vowel chart. This means that the PCT is about equally high but in the back of the mouth near the soft palate instead of in the front of the mouth. The line from the once popular song, "Lookie, lookie, lookie; here comes Cookie!" repeated a number of times before your mirror will fix the audio-visual connection for [ʊ]. In the continuous flux to which language is subject, the [ʊ] and the [u:] are now, in many cases, interchangeable. Thus most dictionaries give both [ʊ] and [u] as equally permissible for *hoop, hoof, room, roof, root, soot* and *coop.* Some words have made the change completely from [u] to [ʊ], such as *cook, look, wood, boor, moor.* The list of words spelled with *oo* and pronounced with the stronger, more tense [u:] is still fairly long, however. Words spelled with *-ool,*\* *oon, -oos, -ooz* are correctly pronounced only with [u:].

You will recall that [ɪ], [ɛ] and [ɔ:] become diphthongs when followed by *r* in the same syllable and are in a position of stress within the sentence. These same conditions affect [ʊ] in the same way. In *"Blessed are the poor,"* where we find [ʊ] followed by *r* and in a posi-

---

\*Except *wool.*

tion of stress, [ʊ] becomes the diphthong [ʊɚ] or [ʊə]. But in *"Blessed are the poor in spirit"* [ʊ] is a short, single vowel with the following *r* eliding with the next vowel and initiating a new syllable, so that *"poor in" becomes* [pʊ rɪn], just as "pour it" becomes [pɔ rɪt]. (See the section on [ɔ:], p. 86.)

## [u:] as in CANOE

| IPA | DMS |
|-----|-----|
| [u:] | (o͞o), (ū), (o̤) |

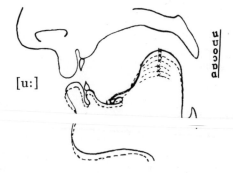

**S P E L L I N G S**

*ru*le, f*ru*it, g*rew*, l*oo*se, d*o*,
tr*ou*pe, d*ue*, d*ew*, man*eu*ver,
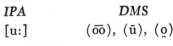

*view.*

[u:]

FIGURE 26

This is the tense, high back vowel made with the PCT humped high in the back of the mouth, almost touching the soft palate, and with the lips tightly rounded. If either of these two shapings of tongue or lips are lazily made, the sound will be colorless and indistinguishable from [ʊ], and certainly not the c*oo*l sound of [u:]. Whenever the spelling contains *u* or *w* (except *ou*) generally the semi-vowel consonant [j] (y) is inserted between the preceding consonant and the vowel, as in *beauty, feud, queue, dew*. Notice the difference as you pronounce these pairs:

| | |
|------|------|
| booty, beauty | coo, cue |
| do, dew | food, feud |
| noon, new | too, tune |
| moo, mew | pool, pew |

It may be noted that [j], (y), is not inserted before [u] if the preceding consonant is *l* or *r*, however.

## TO SUMMARIZE

The sound character of the back vowels is one of larger resonance and darker quality than the front and middle vowels and, consequently, these vowels generally take longer to sound than do the others. To make the back vowels the tongue is humped in the back with a concave, hollow dip in front of the PCT. The three high back vowels must have definitely rounded lip shapes; the lips are tightly pursed for the highest, and relax gradually into larger circles for the next two vowels, then draw down into a vertical oval for the three low back vowels. Now write your sentences containing back vowels for Assignment VIII, p. 82, Part II, *The Work Book*.

From your study and practice of the vowels in these three chapters, you will now have realized that each vowel—front, back or middle— has its own shape and size of opening of the jaw and lips, and its own shape and size of resonance chamber within the mouth made by the gliding back or forward of the PCT. Furthermore, you will have recognized that the vowels are voice; thus, a careful study of the vowels is also a careful study of oral resonance and forward projection of the voice. True and correct vowels will result in clear, well-resonated, well projected tones of voice, pleasant to listen to, easy to understand and will effectively convey meaning.

As you practice for nice distinction of vowels, we would remind you again to concentrate on fixing the muscular sensations with the aural effects. Practice can never be a perfunctory matter, or the results you wish for will elude you.

✿    ✿    ✿

"The elongated, flat vowel sounds that emerged from her slightly opened mouth gave her speech, a lazy, inane quality; made me think of 'Lazy Bones sittin' in the sun.'"

—by a student

# PRONUNCIATIONS

## BACK VOWELS

NOTE. Practice reading aloud the sentences in both columns. Sound the vowels as indicated by the IPA symbols, whether correct or not. Listen with concentration to each vowel; fix in your memory the difference between the desirable and the undesirable sounds.

### DESIRABLE

1a. [ɑ:]–*father* [fɑ:ðɚ], *p a l m* [pɑ:m] PCT low in mouth; tip of tongue against lower gum ridge; lips open in fairly large vertical oval, corners in, making large resonance chamber of the mouth for freest, most open sound of all the vowels.

*The psalms* [sɑ:mz] *of that ancient psalmist* [sɑ:mɪst] *were balm* [bɑ:m] *to the souls of the early American farmers* [fɑ:·····].

1b. [ɑ˞·]–*hark* [hɑ˞·:k]; when the vowel is followed by *r*; lift the middle of the tongue slightly to suggest [r] for good General American.*

*Hark* [hɑ˞k] *to the lark* [lɑ˞k] *singing his heart* [hɑ˞t] *out to the morning star* [stɑ˞].

from the free open position of [ɑ] the mouth closes up to [ʊ]; most common diphthong and most often poorly made.

*The owl* [ɑʊl] *said to himself:* "*With never a sound* [sɑʊnd] *I'll go prowling* [prɑʊlɪŋ] *around* [ərɑʊnd]; *a mouse* [mɑʊs] *or two may be found* [fɑʊnd] *o n the ground* [grɑʊnd].

### UNDESIRABLE

1a. [ɑ̃:]; nasalized. Lips open very little; tone held back and allowed to go up into the nose.

*The sight of pa's* [pɑ̃:z] *heavy palm* [pɑ̃:m] *shattered Harvey's* [hɑ̃:ɾviz] *calm* [kɑ̃:m].

1b. [ɑ̃ɾ]–Strong, inverted [ɾ] following a nasalized [ɑ̃].

*The clatter of the animals in the barn yard* [bɑ̃ɾnjɑ̃ɾd] *alarmed* [əlɑ̃ɾmd] *the farmer* [fɑ̃ɾməɾ].

1c. Substitutions for [ɑ] in diphthong [ɑʊ].

–[æʊ] or [aʊ]; low front vowels; flattens the round back vowel; hardens and often nasalizes the vocal tone; common in many parts of the country. [æʊ] an unpleasant substitution; [aʊ] less so.

*Up and down* [dæʊn] *the streets of the town* [tæʊn] *they trudged. The sound* [sæʊnd] *of their loud* [læʊd] *voices echoed from the surrounding* [səræʊndɪŋ] *mountains* [mæʊntɪnz].

---

*ES: *mark* rhymes with *mock*.

2. [ɒ]–*hot* [hɒt], *long* [lɒŋ], *often*
[ɒfn]; shorter, a trifle darker
sound than [ɑ]; these two often
interchanged. Mouth not quite
so open; PCT a trifle higher in
back.

*The jeweled clock* [klɒk] *had
stopped,* [stɒpt] *so Tom* [tɒm]
*locked* [lɒkt] *it up till he could
take it to the watch* [wɒtch]
*maker.*

2. Substitutions for [ɒ]:
— [ɔ]; too dark; u s u a l l y
mouthed, covered, swallowed
tone; generally unclear.

*Off* [ɔf] *and on* [ɔn] *Robbin's*
[rɔbɪnz] *dog* [dɔg] *disappeared,
much to Robbin's* [rɔbɪnz] *sor-
row* [sɔrou].

3a. [ɔ:]–*paw* [pɔ:], *cause* [kɔ:z],
*ball* [bɔ:l]; PCT higher in back;
lips a small vertical oval, not a
circle; voice forward and free.

*The cat walked* [wɔ:kt] *across
the floor* [flɔr] *and paused*
[pɔ:zd] *with claws* [klɔ:z] *out-
stretched before* [bɪfɚ] *the
mouse hole in the corner*
[kɔ˞nɚ].

3a. [ǫ]; inverted; tongue high
against the velum, blocking the
entrance, holding voice back in
throat; vowel covered, indistinct, almost an [o].

*All* [ǫ] *through the fall* [fǫl]
*Paul* [pǫl] *watched* [wǫtʃt] *the
football* [-bǫl] *games.*

3b. [ɔɚ] (GA) or [ɔə] (ES), *more*
[mɔɚ], *door* [dɔɚ]; an off-glide
from back vowel [ɔ] to middle
[ɚ] when *r* follows the vowel.
Make little of the [r]; touch it
and let it go.

*Cora* [kɔrə] *shut the door* [dɔɚ]
*and said, "Don't let Mort* [mɔt]
*hold forth* [fɔθ] *on folklore*
[-lɔɚ]; *he's a bore* [bɔɚ]."

3b. [ǫr]; both vowel and consonant
inverted; the vowel is almost an
[o]; two syllables of mono-
syllabic words. Lips too round;
PCT too high for [ɔ]; blade and
tip of tongue turning sharply up
after the vowel.

*The child poured* [pǫrd] *the
paint on the floor* [flǫr] *then
walked through it to the door*
[dǫr].

3c. [ɔɪ]–*boy* [bɔɪ], *voice* [vɔɪs];
an off-glide diphthong from
back vowel [ɔ] to front [ɪ]; first
vowel is more open than [o],
though *o* is in the spelling. PCT
moves from half-high back to
higher front; corners of mouth
relax and spread from the [ɔ]
vertical oval to horizontal ellipse of [ɪ].

3c. Substitution for [ɔɪ]:
—[oi]; two strong vowels—not
a diphthong—making two syllables of one.

*The small boy* [boi] *had a voice*
[vois] *like a noisy* [noizi] *par-
rot.*

*Raise harp and voices* [vɔɪsɪz];
*make a joyful* [dʒɔɪ-] *noise*
[nɔɪz] *unto the Lord.*

4a. [o] — *focus* [fokəs], *motor*
[motɚ] *hotel* [hotɛl]; lips
rounded but not too tightly;
PCT in back, tip on floor of
mouth below front teeth.

*With his telephoto* [-foto] *lens
focused* [fokəst] *on the hotel*
[hotɛl]*entrance he hoped [hopt]
to get a picture of the poet*
[poɪt].

4a. Substitutions for [o]:
—[ʊ] in stressed syllables;
—[ə] in unstressed syllables.

*The photo* [fʊtə] *of the finish
of the race showed* [ʃʊd] *the
local* [lʊkəl] *jockey on the win-
ner, Cocoa* [kʊkʊ] *Butter.*

4b. [oʊ]—*dough* [doʊ], *go* [goʊ];
the diphthong in monosyllable
words or in held or stressed
positions. Glide from the more
relaxed rounded lips of [o] to
~~the tighter~~ ~~~~ ~~~~ PCT
half high to high back.

*Go* [goʊ] *by the slower* [sloʊɚ],
*smaller boat* [boʊt], *even
though* [ðoʊ] *it rolls* [roʊlz]
*more.*

4b. Substitution for [oʊ]:
—[ɛo]; an on-glide; lips in the
shape of [ɛ] are pushed out and
rounded while vowel is sounding; PCT also starts with [ɛ]
~~front position~~ and is pulled
back, sliding into [ʊ]; ~~sounds~~
affected and supercilious.

*Oh* [ɛo] *no* [nɛo]! *He couldn't
over-* [ɛovɚ-] *look such a bold*
[bɛold] *attack, you know* [nɛo].

5a. [ʊ]—*foot* [fʊt], *would* [wʊd];
a short, light sound; PCT high
in back; lips fairly tightly
~~held~~

*The brook* [brʊk] *would* [wʊd]
*seem to murmur, "Look* [lʊk],
*look* [lʊk], *every foot* [fʊt] *of
my sparkling pure* [pjʊ] *waters
proclaims the Spring.*

5a. [ʊʊ]; drawled; two distinct
vowels, especially before *l*; the
American drawl, so-called.

*Put* [pʊʊt] *the nail on the hook*
[hʊʊk], *~~drop it down~~ ~~~~ ~~~~
then pull* [pʊʊl] *it up full*
[fʊʊl] *of water.*

5b. [ʊɚ] (GA) or [ʊə] (ES), *poor*
[pʊɚ], *lure* [lʊɚ]; off-glide to
neutral vowel position plus the
suggestion of the [r] for General American; without the
slight [r] for Eastern Standard.

5b. [ʊɻ]; inverted [ɻ] following the
vowel; tip and blade of tongue
turn sharply up; Midwestern
regional drawl.

*Your* [jʊɻ] *soft drink's a poor*
[pʊɻ] *substitute for pure* [pjʊɻ]
*cold water; that's for sure* [ʃʊɻ].

*To be poor* [puɚ] *has no allure*
[əluɚ]; *it is pure* [pjuɚ] *misery*
*with little chance of a cure*
[kjuɚ].

5c. Substitutions for [uɚ]:
—[ɪɹ]; regional dialect; ignor-
ance, or careless habits.

*For pure* [pjɪɹ] *cussedness,*
*you're* [jɪɹ] *sure* [ʃɪɹ] *the top.*

6. [u:]—*pool* [pu:l], *rule* [ru:l],
*few* [fju:]; tightly rounded lips;
PCT high in back.

*The two* [tu:] *little Pooles*
[pu:lz], *Beulah* [bju:lə] *and*
*Luie* [lu:i], *went moose* [mu:s]
*hunting in the zoo* [zu:].

6a. [uu] or [uə]; double vowels, or
diphthongized by off-glide;
failure to hold PCT high in
back, especially before *l.* Another instance of American
drawl.

*In school* [skuul] *you* [ju:] *must*
*follow the rules* [ruulz].

6b. [iu]; on glide; lips in thin line
of [i] are pursed into tight
circle of [u]; PCT at first high
front, then pulled back tensely;
usually nasalized unpleasantly,
also.

*Eat your* [jɪɹ] *soup,* [siup] *Jun-*
*ior* [dʒiunɪɹ], *then put on your*
[jɪɹ] *shoes* [ʃiuz] *and go to*
*school* [skiul].

NOTE. Now begin Assignment IX, the Back Vowels you habitually
mispronounce, p. 84, Part II, the *Work Book.* Like Assignments V
and VII, this is a continuing assignment. Make the most of each for
your own speech improvement.

# Chapter XI

## Articulating the Consonants

If speech is civilization itself, as we are told, then it must be easily understood speech that projects ideas and moves civilization forward. "Except ye utter by the tongue words easy to understand, how shall it be known what is spoken?"* asked that early philosopher. That, indeed, is the whole concern of our study: how to perfect the physical mechanics of articulation in order that our words be easily understood. Furthermore, it is consonants that give intelligibility to speech, according to that great teacher, Alexander Graham Bell. "Consonants constitute the back-bone of spoken language—vowels the flesh and blood," he said in his picturesque way. We shall now give attention to the twenty-three consonants of our language, which "give intelligibility to speech."

It would be revealing and doubtless amusing if we could know what our speech would sound like if we ignored the consonants of the words we speak. Here is a sketch† which suggests phonetically what all too frequently happens to speech when consonants—and sometimes vowels— are ignored. Read the sketch aloud. Do you hear yourself in the speech of Mr. and Mrs. Joe Enslow? They are "sitting in their typical Murcan home, talking in their typical Murcan way about the wunnerful meyum of ennertainmen, television."

"Joe, a table moll set doesn't cos much, an we coul pay for it on the monthly installmen plan."

"Lisn, swee, I think TV is harbul."

"Oh, Joe! It's really triffic. You havn seen it enough. It's a great monumum to marn progress. An the churun woul love it."

"Well, I think it's tairbul. Domnates the livin room; all plite conversation stops, and you have to feed the whol nayerhood."

*I Corinthians 14:9. See Frontispiece.
†By Nancy Dallam Sinkler in *Post Script*, THE SATURDAY EVENING POST, March 31, 1951.

"You're so reactionary, Joe. Your thinking ough to go ford. The mistry and tective plays are tops and you'd love Miln Berle. He's aslutely sterical."

"I woul not. Watching TV gives me a stigmatism a nralgia!"

"Your nralgia is jus motional. You jus have a block."

"Awri, so I'm blocked, so I have to fin out what lectronics did to my mother, maybe? It wasn even vented then!"

"All men like the spors evens and the plitical speeches. I'd like to watch the Nited Nations sessions myself, an when you're away on bisness trips and lee me lone, it woul keep me company."

"Thisis a losin bal."

"Oh, Joe, please, le's ge one home just on proval an try it."

"Nuts! Go ahead an ge it. I jus deman one thing."

"Cernly, dear, What?"

"A quiet spot somewhere for me where I can sell down with a goo book."

Not only are many of the consonant "backbones" missing in this gem of Americana, but the "flesh and blood" vowels are often emasculated, as well, and whole syllables disappear. Let this not be said of your speech. Consonants do make for intelligibility; otherwise, there is merely mouthed, not articulated, sound. It follows, then, that consonants must be neatly enunciated, be clean-cut, and have their correct proportion of sound to the vowels. Obviously, to make twenty-five vowels clearly particularized and twenty-five consonants neatly correct, the tongue must be very flexible from tip to back. Flexibility of the tongue is attained by purposeful practice. To this end use Exercises III and IV in the *Work Book,* pp. 101-103, vigorously and often.

## THERE ARE FOUR CLASSIFICATIONS OF CONSONANTS

We have already pointed out (Chapter 6) that the vocal stream of the vowel (the sonant) is interrupted either partially or completely by some action of the tongue or lips or, in one instance, of the vocal bands themselves; and the effect is a lesser sound which we call a consonant. According to these actions we may classify consonants in four ways.

1. *As to the amount of interruptions of the breath stream.* To make consonants the breath stream is either completely shut off or impeded. For six consonants it is abruptly cut off by making a dam of the tongue or lips. These are called STOP consonants. For the rest the breath stream is only partially interrupted; these seventeen consonants are known as CONTINUANTS.

2. *As to the manner of interrupting the breath stream.* This factor gives a particular quality of sound to the consonants. In the six stop consonants air is released suddenly (the PLOSIVES); in three consonants there is a distinctive nasal hum from the air diverted into nasal passages (the NASALS); for one consonant the air escapes along the sides of the tongue (the LATERAL); twelve others have a quality of friction from impeding the passage of the breath through the mouth (the FRICATIVES), of which three are part vowel, part consonant (the SEMIVOWELS).

3. *As to the focal point of action within the mouth.* The lips are involved in making seven (the LABIALS). The tongue comes into contact with the teeth for two more—and only two— (the DENTALS), in contact with or proximity to the upper gum ridge for nine others (the ALVEOLARS), and with the palate for three more (the PALATAL and the VELARS). There is a slight involvement of the glottis in the making of the aspirate consonant *h* (the GLOTTAL).

4. *As voiced or voiceless.* For some consonants the glottis is narrowed to a tiny slit, the vocal bands vibrate and voice is generated, producing the VOICED consonants. There are other consonants produced with no vibration of the vocal bands; they are the UNVOICED, or VOICELESS, consonants. In eight instances you will note that the voiced and voiceless consonants occur in pairs; each twin is made with identical action within the mouth, but one has vocal vibrations while the other is voiceless.

As we have seen, all the vowels are voice, and each is the particular vocal sound of a particular resonance chamber made within the mouth, until it is interrupted in a particular manner by a particular consonant. FIGURE 27 on the following page will indicate how the consonants are articulated. Study the chart carefully and familiarize yourself with the IPA symbols.

# FOCAL POINT AND MANNER OF ARTICULATION

| MANNER OF ARTICULATION →INTERRUPTIONS OF THE BREATH STREAM | AMOUNT OF INTERRUPTIONS OF THE BREATH STREAM | LABIAL — Both lips | | LABIAL — Upper teeth on lower lip | | DENTAL — Tip of tongue to teeth | | ALVEOLAR — Tip of tongue on or near upper gumridge | | ALVEOLAR — Blade of tongue near upper gumridge | | PALATAL — Middle or front of T. to hard palate | | VELAR — Back of tongue to soft palate | | GLOTTAL — Air through the closed glottis | |
|---|---|---|---|---|---|---|---|---|---|---|---|---|---|---|---|---|---|
| | | Unv.[1] | V[2] | Unv. | V | Unv. | V | Unv. | V | Unv. | V | Unv. | V | Unv. | V | Unv. | V |
| PLOSIVE | STOPS | [p] | [b] | | | | | [t] | [d] | | | | | [k] | [g] | | |
| NASAL | CONTINUANTS | | [m] | | | | | | [n] | | | | | | [ŋ] | | |
| LATERAL | CONTINUANTS | | | | | | | | [l] | | | | | | | | |
| FRICATIVE | CONTINUANTS | [ʍ]³ | [w]⁴ | [f] | [v] | [θ] | [ð] | [s]⁵ | [z]⁵ [r]⁴·⁵ | [ʃ]⁵ [tʃ] | [ʒ]⁵ [dʒ] | | [j]⁴ | | | [h] | |

FIGURE 27
PHONETIC CHART OF CONSONANTS

1. Unvoiced or Voiceless.    2. Voiced.    3. Sometimes written [hw].    4. Also called semi-vowels.

5. For these, the tongue is near, but not touching the gumridge.

Doubtless you already recognize many of the phonetic symbols for the consonants. Most of those that are strange appear in the Fricative row, with the exception of the third nasal, [ŋ], and the third semi-vowel, [j]. Note the extension of the leg of the *n* in making [ŋ] which is the sound frequently spelled by *ng*. The [j] consonant on the chart does not represent the sound of *j* in *judge*, but rather the sound of *j* in the German word *ja*, which is the sound of *y* in *yellow*. Among the fricative consonants the first strange symbol is the voiceless [ʍ] made by turning the *w* upside down, and sometimes written [hw]. Since it is voiceless, it has no vowel-like character as does its twin voiced [w], which is often called a semivowel. The next two strange symbols among the Fricatives are the twin dental *th* sounds. As you see on the chart (Figure 27), the symbol for the dental voiceless *th*, [θ], in *thin* is the Greek Theta while the voiced *th*, [ð], in *then* is the Anglo-Saxon Edh, which appears as something of a modified, crossed *d*. In the next box the sibilants [s] and [z] are familiar, but the symbol [ʃ] for *sh* as in *hush* and the symbol [ʒ] for the *z* in *azure* are less so, though some of you will recognize the [ʃ] as the _____ in German. Practice writing and sounding all the consonants until you are very familiar with them and can write them quickly from dictation.

# TECHNIQUES OF VOICE INFLUENCE CONSONANTS

Once again we would call attention to the fact that the study of the techniques of voice production are pertinent to all phases of articulation. This we have already seen in respect to vowels. In the articulation of consonants breath control, particularly over the amount and force of the breath, is very important. Lack of breath control results in over-aspiration and is especially noticeable in the case of the Fricatives. Too much breath makes them too heavy and too long, often to the point of obscuring the vowel following. Test your own enunciation of [f] in this line from *The Tempest*: "Full fathom five thy father lies," and of the [s] in this from *Mother Goose*: "Sing a song of sixpence," or this from Amy Lowell: "Sea shells, sea shells, sing me a song, O please." Does the breath seem to push hard against the teeth and lips with each [f] or [s]? Can you hear air escaping noisily through the dam of your lips? Then there is too much force of breath being used. Read these lines again with the lightest touch of breath, just enough to generate voice for the vowel, no more. This is particularly important for the initial [s] consonant. The [s] is the noisiest of all consonants and care must be taken to make it light of breath, or the heaviness of the sibilant will assail the ears of the listener harshly, may cover the vowel and make understanding more difficult. The rule of breath in respect to consonants should be to touch initial consonants very lightly, articulating them simultaneously with the vowel following. Most of the power of breath should be used to voice the vowels. Exercise VIII-C in the *Work Book*, Part I, p.42, is particularly pertinent here. Take note of Direction 3, especially.

## THE ARTICULATORS MUST BE FLEXIBLE

For vowels the movements of the tongue are smooth, gliding movements of the whole tongue; for consonants the tongue must move lightly, quickly and flexibly in each of its five sections: tip, blade, front, middle and back; each section must be able to work almost independently of the others. For vowels the movements of the jaw and lips are large and strong and have a considerable influence on the quality and clarity of the vowel to be pronounced. For consonants the movements of the jaw and lips are small and light and at a minimum; the tongue is the very active member of the articulators in enunciating consonants. Unfortunately, sluggishness of the articulators, especially of the tongue, is all too common among us, and justifies our being called "lip-lazy and tongue-lazy Americans." Flexibility of the tongue, especially flexibility of the tip of the tongue, is absolutely necessary for fine, clean consonants and neat, intelligible speech. "Flexibility of the tip of the tongue" is an excellent practice phrase in itself to help you gain just what it says. Say it aloud whenever you are alone and listen for the light, clear [ɪ] vowel and the clean, neat [t]; listen, too, for your sounding lightly, but distinctly, each of the eleven syllables that make up the phrase. See Exercise IV, in the *Work Book*, Part II, *p.*103.

## OBSERVATIONS ON THE SPELLING AND PRONOUNCING OF CONSONANTS

There are a few observations to be made on the spelling and pronunciation of consonants that can be helpful in our study. The most important is that when there are two consonants together in the same syllable, they will both be of the same classification of sound, both voiced or both unvoiced, the second taking its character from the first. To know when a consonant is voiced, place your thumb and finger on either side of your "Adam's apple" and pronounce the first consonant. If you feel vibration the consonant is voiced; if you feel no vibration the consonant is unvoiced. Pronounce: *starts and stops*. Finger-test the *st, ts,* and *ps.* Finger-test also: *deeds* [didz], *flamed* [flemd]; the final letters *s* and *d* are the voiced [z] and [d], influenced by the voiced character of their respective preceding consonants.

Consider these pairs of verbs all ending in *-ed;* in the first column the *d* is voiceless and pronounced [t] following an unvoiced consonant; in the second column in which the *d* follows a voiced consonant it is voiced and pronounced [d].

| | |
|---|---|
| supped [sʌpt] | sobbed [sɒbd] |
| stopped [stɒpt] | stabbed [stæbd] |
| lacked [lækt] | lagged [lægd] |
| dosed [dost] | dozed [doʊzd] |
| laced [lest] | lazed [leizd] |
| groped [gʳ·ᵖ·] | ~~~~ [gʳ·ᵖbd] |
| clocked [klɒkt] | clogged [klɒgd] |

At this point do Assignment X, p. 85, Part II of the *Work Book.*

Consider, also, the words below, all ending in *s.* In the first column the *s* is voiceless and pronounced [s] following an unvoiced consonant or a short vowel; in the second column in which the *s* follows a voiced consonant or a long vowel, the *s* is pronounced [z].

| | |
|---|---|
| boots [buts] | ~~~~ [bᵉᵃdz] |
| bits [bɪts] | beads [bi:dz] |
| geese [gis] | trees [tri:z] |
| case [kes] | days [deɪz] |
| knacks [næks] | nags [nægz] |
| writes [raɪts] | rides [raɪdz] |
| dose [dos] | pose [po:z] |

Now do Assignment XI, Part II of the *Work Book,* p. 86.

In English spelling one frequently sees two or more consonants in a word pronounced as one, and sometimes the same combination of letters represents two, even three, different consonants. In Chapter 7 we took incidental note of the erratic behavior of *gh* in such words as *rough* [rʌf], *trough* [trɔ:θ], *though* [ðou]. *Pn* in pneumonia, pneumatic, etc. are familiar enough spellings for the single sound [n], as are *gn* in *gnat* and *kn* in *know; th*, as we have noted above, is sometimes pronounced [θ], sometimes [ð] and sometimes [t] as in *Thames*—[tɛmz] and *thyme*—[taɪm]; *ph* pronounced as [f] is familiar in many words—*sphere, phonetic, telephone*. Less familiar are mnemonic [nimɒnɪk], phthisic [tɪzɪk]. These mysteries of English spelling and pronunciation seem to have no rhyme or reason, and the dictionary remains our best guide in their pronunciation. They remind us that our language has its roots in many languages, which fact accounts for the multiple spellings of many vowel and consonant sounds.

In your study of the consonant chart (Figure 27) you doubtless noticed that while there are both familiar and strange symbols, there are still some familiar letters of the orthographic alphabet which do not appear in the phonetic alphabet. These are *c, q, x* and *y*. The letter *c* is sometimes pronounced [k] and sometimes [s] as in *cat*—[kæt] and *cite*—[saɪt]; *y* is sometimes the consonant semivowel [j] in *yet*—[jɛt], sometimes the pure vowel [ɪ] in *hymn*—[hɪm] or sometimes the diphthong [aɪ] as in *sky*—[skaɪ]; *q* is phonetically [k].

There is no letter *x*, in phonetic script because *x* is a combination of two other sounds, the combination having two separate phonetic values: the voiceless [ks] in *expect*—[ɛkspɛkt], and the voiced [gz] in *exalt*—[ɛgzɔ:lt]. At this point we should note that in general *x* is the voiceless [ks] but that it becomes the voiced [gz] when the *x* is followed by a stressed syllable beginning with a vowel. To illustrate, *exit* is pronounced [ɛksɪt], not [ɛgzɪt], because the following syllable, though beginning with a vowel, is unstressed; *examine* is pronounced [ɛgzæmɪn], not [ɛksæmɪn], because *x* precedes a stressed syllable beginning with a vowel.

The so-called "soft g" is actually two sounds [dʒ] which we sometimes see spelled with a *j* as in *jaw*, sometimes spelled *ge* as in *age* [eɪdʒ]. The sound of *ch*, as in *church*, is also two sounds, [tʃ]. You will notice that these last two combinations, [dʒ] and [tʃ], are voiced and voiceless twins.

## TO SUMMARIZE

While vowels are the voice, consonants are interruptions of the voice-vowel stream. With the vowels they create the syllables that make the words that give language meaning. In the making of consonants we observe that they are the result of breath, voiced or unvoiced, emitted under various conditions, making various characters of sound by completely stopping or only partially interrupting the breath. For the livliest speaking and the greatest understandability flexible, clean-cut action of the articulators, especially of the tongue in each of its sections, is absolutely necessary. Substitutions, slurring or dropping of consonants, reduce and sometimes completely destroy intelligibility.

Finally, it must be remembered that the techniques of breath control, so important in the development of good voice and the oral resonance of good vowels are also important in the articulation of consonants, particularly those techniques of control over the amount and force of the exhaled breath stream.

# GLOSSARY

## THE CONSONANTS

| DESIRABLE | UNDESIRABLE |
|---|---|
| 1. *CLEAN-CUT CONSONANTS.* True articulation of consonants; invariably the result of flexible, neat actions of the tongue and lips. | 1. *SLOVENLY CONSONANTS.* Unintelligible blurs of articulation; omission rather than emission of consonants; even a swallowing of whole syllables. |

*DESIRABLE*

1. *CLEAN-CUT CONSONANTS.* True articulation of consonants; invariably the result of flexible, neat actions of the tongue and lips.

"His speech is most beautifully like sculpture—not a syllable slurred or scarred."
—of John Gielgud's Hamlet
—by Sydney Porter

2a. *LIGHTLY BREATHED CONSONANTS.* In combinations with vowels consonants enunciated very lightly with minimum amount of breath, never overshadowing the vowels.

"Her c l e a r, well-modulated voice read of James James Morrison M o r r i s o n Weatherby George Dupres as though there were a tiny elf in her mouth, playfully tossing out her words with neat flicks of his wand, delicately exploding her *t*'s and *d*'s, lightly tuning her *m*'s and *n*'s and delightfully minding her *p*'s and *q*'s."
—by a student

2b. *SHORT CONSONANTS.* Consonants short in proportion to the timing of vowels; initial consonants sounded almost simultaneously with the following vowel; final consonants dropped as soon as sounded.

*UNDESIRABLE*

1. *SLOVENLY CONSONANTS.* Unintelligible blurs of articulation; omission rather than emission of consonants; even a swallowing of whole syllables.

"Mrs. Joe Elision, talking about her forthcoming vacation: 'I wanna go to Nyork, Joe. I wanna get some new cloes an some garn furncher an go to niclubs an the opra an eat lobster Newburg an have a really high-par time.' "
—Nancy Dallam Sinkler

2a. *OVER-ASPIRATED.* H e a v y, fuzzy consonants; result of too much audible breath pushed with too much force against the teeth and lips, especially on initial consonants.

"His speech was remarkable for the force of breath with which he blew out every word as if it were a candle."
—by a student

2b. *TOO LONG.* C o n s o n a n t s drawn out as long as, or longer than, the vowels; occurs most frequently with final [m], [n] and [r]; initial [s] often anticipated and final [s] held too long.

"The child loved to hear her delicate, light enunciation of the words so much that he repeated the lines after her with the same short, fine hiss of the *s*, the same light touch on the other consonants and the same true vowel sounds:

'Of speckled eggs the birdie sings
And nests among the trees;
The sailor sings of ropes and things
In ships upon the seas.'"
—by a student

"Savoring the feel of his tongue turning and rolling in his mouth, he spoke in one long blur of *r*'s. But whenever he said the word 'money', which he did quite frequently, the *m* and *n* melted into each other in one long caress, as if he were loath to let go even of the thought."
—by a student

"A loudly hissing *s* spat at me, serpent-like, from every sentence. But as she continued to speak, h i s s i n g steadily, I thought: It is merely a leaking tire and soon will be entirely flat."
—by a student

# Chapter XII

---

## The Plosives, Nasals, and Lateral "L"

---

Let us now begin to consider the consonants of our English-American language, one by one, as we did the vowels, remembering that together they make the syllables of the words with which we express ourselves. Fine, clean consonants instantly make the word intelligible, while the full clarity of the vowels gives it significance. We must constantly remind ourselves that the clarity of the vowels, however, is possible only if the consonants that bracket the vowels are neatly articulated with the utmost flexibility of the articulators, especially of the tongue.

## THE PLOSIVES

| BI-LABIAL | | ALVEOLAR | | VELAR | |
|---|---|---|---|---|---|
| Unv | V | Unv | V | Unv | V |
| p | b | t | d | k | g |

FIGURE 28

To make the consonants of this first group, completely stop the flow of breath in the mouth, then release it immediately with a slight, explosive sound; hence the name of these consonants: PLOSIVES. As you see by the chart (Fig. 27), three key places in the mouth are involved in making these six consonants: the lips, the upper gum ridge (ALVEOLAR ARCH) and the soft palate (VELUM). To make [t–d] and [k–g], the tongue is involved with the gum ridge and the soft palate: [p–b], the lips only are involved.

*THE BI-LABIAL PLOSIVES:* [p] as in *PAT, CAP, PAPER*
[b] as in *BALL, CAB, DUBIOUS*

*IPA DMS*
1. [p]  (p) Unvoiced
2. [b]  (b) Voiced

S P E L L I N G S
1. *p*en, *pe*p*p*er
2. *b*all, *bobb*in

To make [p] and [b] bring both lips together, stopping the flow of breath at the most forward point within the mouth, just before it is emitted from the oral chamber. Now release the breath with a very slight plosive aspiration. Practicing these consonants made so far forward on the lips can be helpful toward acquiring the very important vocal technique of forward projection. Pronounce slowly: *Peter Piper picked a peck of pickled peppers.* Notice how clearly the vowel sounds emerge after the [p], seeming to be lightly exploded with the [p] and falling neatly over the lips. Sound the line again listening for the clear vowel sounds this time. Once more we may note the interrelation of voice and speech. For the sake of neatness in articulation as well as clarity of voice we must acquire controls over the amount and force of breath. While the lips should be ~~~~~~ ~~~~ to make [p] and [b] they must not be too tight and tense or the explosive release of the breath will be too heavy and noisy. Make sure that the final [p] or [b], especially, as in *cap* or *cab*, is light with merely a touch of breath in the short plosive: *cab* [kæb], not [kæbə].

*THE ALVEOLAR PLOSIVES:* [t] as in *TYPE, HAT, MOUNTAIN*
[d] as in *DO, BAD, FOLDER*

*IPA DMS*
1. [t]  (t) Unvoiced
2. [d]  (d) Voiced

S P E L L I N G S
1. *t*ype, gli*tt*er, *t h* y m e, look*ed*, eigh*t*.
2. *d*o, fo*dd*er, stow*ed*

To make a clean-cut, neatly plosive [t] or [d] stop ~~~ ~~~~ ~~~~ at the gum ridge with a flick of the tongue to the ridge, then drop the tongue straight down releasing the breath with a light plosive effect. Too often we hear a sibilant-like fricative sound instead of a neat plosive effect of [t] or [d] when the tip of the tongue touches the teeth rather than the upper gum ridge behind and above the teeth. The movement of the tongue for this pair of consonants is a "plunger action" up and down, not a "piston-rod movement" forward and back. We now begin to be concerned with the flexibility of the tip of the tongue even more than of the whole tongue.

These consonants often appear in final combinations with other consonants: [kt] as in *fact* and [gd] in *bagged;* [pt] in *stopped* and [bd] in *robbed;* [st] in *last* and [zd] in *gazed;* [ft] in *raft* and [vd] in *lived.* Notice that these consonants in combination are always of the same voice classification, both unvoiced—[pt], [kt], [st]—or both voiced— [bd], [gd], [zd], [vd], etc. It is not too difficult for a flexible tongue to enunciate these combinations of consonants neatly. It is not easy, however, in rapid conversational speech to make combinations of three consonants, such as the [kts] in *acts* or the [sts] in *lists.* As a consequence the [t] is frequently lost in these words.

Not only do careless speakers with inflexible tongues drop the final [t], but they frequently glottalize the medial [t] by stopping the breath with tightened vocal bands. The effect of glottalizing a medial [t] is a gutteral, swallowing sound in the middle of such words as *butter, rotted, redden, mountain.* Here again, the techniques of smooth voice production have an important effect on speaking to insure the constant forward flow of syllables of speech falling clearly and smoothly on the ear of the listener.

If you do not make neat, clean *t*'s in your speech, practice Exercise XIII of Part II the *Work Book* (p.91) over and over. Exercises IV, V and VII, pp. 103, 105, 107, wil be helpful also.

*THE VELAR PLOSIVES:* [k] as in KEEL, BACK, BASKET
[g] as in GOLD, RAG, FINGER

| IPA | DMS | |
|-----|-----|--|
| 1. [k] | (k) | Unvoiced |
| 2. [g] | (g) | Voiced |

S P E L L I N G S

1. *k*itten, *c*ash, ba*ck*, a*cc*ount, ba*cch*anal, *c h a r a c t e r,* sa*cque*, a*cq*uaint, bis*c*uit, li*qu*or, pi*que*.
2. *g*old, be*gg*ed, *gh*ost, *gu*ide, monolo*gue*.

The focal point of tongue action for these consonants is the back, soft part of the palate where the tongue firmly touches the velum, effectively stopping the breath as it enters the mouth. As with the other plosive consonants there is a slight pause before the tongue is removed with a quick, sudden action to make the plosive character of the consonant.

Again breath control must be employed, not only over the amount to prevent breathiness when the consonants are released, but also over the direction of the breath up out of the throat and forward into the mouth. With [k] and [g] there is danger of the breath being stopped in the larynx by a glottal stop rather than a velar stop just inside the mouth.

A glottal plosive, as we have noted, has a harsh, gutteral quality which sounds as if the speaker were "clearing his throat," rather than the light, neat, clean-cut quality all consonants should have.

Now write the sentences for the Plosives in Assignment XII of Part II (p. 87), the *Work Book.*

## THE NASALS

| BI-LABIAL | | ALVEOLAR | | VELAR | |
|---|---|---|---|---|---|
| Unv | V | Unv | V | Unv | V |
| | m | | n | | ŋ |

FIGURE 29

These three nasal consonants are the first of the four groups of CONTINUANTS (See Figure 27, Chapter 11) that we shall consider. Note in Figures 28 and 29 that the same places within the mouth are involved in making the plosive consonants and the nasal consonants. In addition to the voiced nasal hum of the latter group, the difference between the Nasals [m], [n], and [ŋ], and the Plosives, [ ], [ ], [ ], lies in the manner of releasing the lips and the tongue. Instead of exploding the tongue from its position on the gum ridge or the velum, gently ease it off to make the Nasals.

*THE BI-LABIAL NASAL:* [m] as in MAD, RAM, HAMLET

*IPA*   *DMS*
[m]   (m) Voiced

mark, mammal, palm, diaphragm, bomb, hymn, brougham.

[m] is made by closing the oral chamber at the lips and allowing the breath to hum around in both the oral and nasal chamber. The tongue and the oral chamber are quite as relaxed as for the neutral vowel [ə] and in fact are physiologically equivalent, with the breath stream flowing through the mouth shaped for the vowel but through the nasal passage for the [m]. From the initial [m] the lips gradually open into the shape for the following vowel. A final [m] is held only until the next consonant initiating a new syllable is articulated. The [m] must be released the instant the articulators move into another position. Recall here the exercise of [m<ɑ:] (Exercise VI Pt. I of the *Work Book*, p. 37); the closed-mouth [m] gradually opens into the full resonance of the vowel [ɑ:], running the complete line of back vowels from [u:] to [ɑ:]. Recall, also, the line of syllables beginning

with [m] in the "Train Call" exercise (Ex. VIII, Pt. I, p. 41). You were admonished to drop the [m] immediately you sounded the vowel in each syllable of [mɑ: meɪ mi: maɪ moʊ mu:]; again in the "Conversation Piece" exercise using the same syllables (Ex. XV, Pt. II, p. 112 ). Just so in any conversational speech, an initial nasal consonant must be dropped as soon as it is articulated so as to allow the following vowel clear resonance in the oral chamber. Neither is it good to prolong a final nasal consonant for any length of time. When a speaker holds on to a final [m] or [n] he gives the impression of being "in love with the sound of his own voice" to the exclusion of meaningfulness of expression.

### THE ALVEOLAR NASAL: [n] as in NOD, RUN, FINAL

*IPA    DMS*
[n]    (n) Voiced

*S P E L L I N G S*
now, pneumonia, gnat,
know, funny.

This second nasal consonant, [n], is made with the articulators in exactly the same positions as for the plosive [d]. The difference in the production of these two sounds lies entirely in the action of the tongue upon the breath stream. As we have seen in the case of [d], a flick of the tongue away from the alveolar ridge produces a sudden release of the damned up breath stream. For [n] the tongue lies steadily on the gum ridge while the breath stream travels in an even, constant flow, escaping partly through the oral chamber and partly through the nasal passage.

In pronouncing such words as *fine, mind, lane, lean,* care must be taken not to anticipate the final [n]. This nasalizes the vowel preceding the [n] and the result is an unpleasant whining quality of sound. Again you are admonished to drop the initial [n] the instant you sound the following vowel; and although the final [n] is usually a little longer than the initial [n], it, too, should not be prolonged for any length of time, to avoid the risk of sounding pedantic and supercilious.

### THE VELAR NASAL: [ŋ] as in SING, SINGER, SINGLE

*IPA    DMS*
[ŋ]    (ng) Voiced

*S P E L L I N G S*
tongue, sing, think, lynx,
uncle, anchor, conquer.

This third nasal consonant, [ŋ], is made with the tongue humped high against the velum as in making [g]. The breath stream, however, flows steadily without interruption partly through the nasal passage, partly around the high hump of the tongue and out through the slightly open mouth. [ŋ] is a medial or final consonant; it never begins a word. If the spelled word ends in *ng*, the final sound is always [ŋ], as in *song* [sɒŋ] *swing* [smɪŋ], *hang* [hæŋ]. Remember that in making the final [ŋ] the tongue is released from the velum in a smooth, easy action, not suddenly and plosively. Even when derivatives are formed from verbs ending in *ng*, as *singer* and *singing*, the *ng* still remains [ŋ], and the words are [sɪŋɚ], [sɪŋɪŋ].

There are, however, two instances when *ng* becomes [ŋg]. In the first the *g* is sounded after the [ŋ] when the suffixes *-er* and *-est* are added to the three adjectives ending in *ng*, *long* [lɒŋ], *strong* [strɒŋ], and *young* [jʌŋ], to form the comparative and superlative forms; e.g., [lɒŋ], [lɒŋgɚ], [strɒŋ]–[strɒŋgɚ], [jʌŋ]–[jʌŋgɪst]. In the second instance, if *ng* falls in the middle of a word, as in *single, finger, language,* both [ŋ] and [g] are heard and we have [sɪŋgl], [fɪŋgɚ], [læŋgwɪdʒ]. *Gangster, gingham, Birmingham* and all words ending in *ngham*, are exceptions: [gæŋstɚ], [gɪŋəm], [bɝmɪŋhəm].

In many words when a prefix ends in *n*, and *g* begins a new syllable, as *congratulate*, *ungratejur*, .... ........ ..............ed as an alveolar nasal [n] and the g as a hard velar plosive [g]. When in spelling the wu.. ... g is followed by *e* we have phonetically a quite different circumstance; here the *g* is not [g] but two other sounds, [dʒ], which exert no influence upon the preceding *n*. Thus *hinge* is  hɪndʒ]; *lounge* is [laʊndʒ].

Then there are words ending in *nk, nx*, as *monk, bank, lynx*. In such words the letter *n* is pronounced [ŋ], which is followed by the plosive [k]: [mʌŋk], [bæŋk], [lɪŋks].

... .... .......... .....RAL: [l] as in LATE, RAIL, WILDER

| | |
|---|---|
| *IPA*   *DMS* | Occupying a whole classiﬁ..... ¹ . |
| [l]    (1) Voiced | itself this lone lateral consonant is so-called because the strongly vocalized |
| S P E L L I N G S | breath rolls off the sides of the tongue |
| wi*l*d. wi*ll*. | in the sounding of it. The tip of the |

tongue touches firmly on the edge of the alveolar arch at the point where the hard palate begins to arch up from the ridge, diverting the vocal stream over the sides of the tongue. This would seem to be a simple action of the tongue, easy and uncomplicated, yet many children learning to talk seem to be unable to find the place for the tongue to sound [l] and frequently substitute some other consonant for it, [w] or [j] (y), as in the word *look*, pronouncing it [wʊk] or [jʊk].

The [l] varies in the amount of sound it has in it depending on where it falls in a word. It is short and light, a "clear *l*" so-called, if it is either the initial or the second consonant in a word, as in *last* or *class;* it is a "dark *l*," longer and fuller, if it is the final or next to a final consonant, as in *will* or *cold.* Be careful not to insert a second vowel before the final dark [l], as in the word *rule,* for example. This would affect a kind of drooling drawl. Beware the tendency to drawl.

These two slightly different sounds for the consonant *l* are acceptable in good American speech, but an inverted\* [ḷ], made with the tip of the tongue turned back toward the soft palate, is not good. It produces a sound that is dull and covered, preventing clarity not only to itself but to the vowels that precede or follow. Furthermore, an inverted [ḷ] is also likely to be nasalized, an extremely unpleasant sound. Inversion is to be avoided at all times.

At this point write your sentences for the nasal and lateral consonants in Assignment XXII, Part II, p. 88 the *Work Book.*

## TO SUMMARIZE

While the Plosive and the Nasal consonants are so very different in sound effect, it is interesting to note that in the making of them the same positions of the tongue are used. The manifest difference in the sounds between them lies in the different manner of removing the tongue from those positions plus different techniques of the breath and voice. The Plosive consonants are the result of carefully exploded breath as it is released through the suddenly opened dam of the lips. With the warm Nasals on the other hand, the dam of the lips is kept closed and the stream of voice is diverted through the nasal passages. You must remember in your practice of the nasal consonants, however, that only the consonants are nasalized, not the vowels that precede or follow them. Techniques of voice and breath control must operate on these consonants as well as on the vowels. The *m* and *n* lines of Exercise XV, Part II p. 112, the *Work Book* are excellent for these techniques. Work for flexibility of the tongue and the lips as well as fine timing of the voice. Vow to yourself that you will make yourself easily understood.

---

\*To indicate an inversion with IPA symbols, put a dot (.) below the consonant.

# PRONUNCIATIONS

## THE PLOSIVES, NASALS, AND THE LATERAL "L"

NOTE. Practice reading aloud the sentences below in both columns. Deliberately sound the consonants as indicated by the IPA symbols, whether you know them to be correct or not. Listen with concentration to each consonant you make and fix in your memory the difference between the desirable and the undesirable sounds. You will, of course, give careful attention to the vowels as well.

### DESIRABLE

1. [p]–*pie* [paɪ]; the breath is stopped at the lips; released suddenly with a light, easy plosive sound of unvoiced air.

   *Please* [pliːz] *put* [pʊt] *the* ˡ~ ⌐~ˡˡ *on the plate* [plet].

2. [b]–*bat* [bæt]–the voiced twin of [p]; a heavier sound with voice added.

   *A bat* [bæt] *and ball* [bɔːl] *were bought* [bɔːt] *for each boy* [bɔɪ].

3. [t]–*tone* [toʊn]–the breath ˙‒‒‒⌐ ɑt ơm ridge by tip of tongue; released suddenly cleanly by dropping tongue straight down into position for next vowel or consonant.

   *Little* [lɪtl] *Tommy* [tɒmɪ] *Townesend* [taʊnzənd] *tinkers* [tɪŋkɚz] *with his toys* [tɔɪz].

### UNDESIRABLE

1. [pʰ]–*pole* [pʰol]–too heavy breath escapes after the [p] is released.

   *Pull* [pʰʊl], *boys, pull* [pʰʊl]; *altogether now, pull* [pʰʊl] *away.*

2. ⌐-bəˡ–*cab* [ræ~~ʲ] ated final [b]; too much force of voiced breath exploding the [b] into a full syllable with the neutral vowel following, [bə]. *There's nothing drab* [dræbə] *about driving a cab* [kæbə].

3a. [t̪]*–dentalized; tip of tongue against teeth; breath released ···ith fricative sound. Not clean-cut; makes ɪ○ı ○····ɪ ‒‒ɑ extra sibilance in the speech.

   *Tell* [t̪ɛl] *Tommy* [t̪ɒmɪ] *to* [t̪ʊ] *stop* [st̪ɒp] *tinkering* [t̪ɪŋkərɪŋ] *with it* [ɪt̪].

3b. [ʔ]–glottalized [t], usually in the middle of words; breath stopped at the glottis; sound seems to be swallowed; guttural quality.

   *He threw the bottle* [bɒʔl] *in the gutter* [gʌʔɚ].

---

*To indicate dentalized speech place [˷] below the IPA symbol as [t̪], [d̪] etc.

4. [d]—*done* [dʌn]; the voiced twin of [t]; a heavier sound with the voice added.

*The dolt* [dolt] *poured* [pɔd] *the Dramboui* [dræmbui] *down* [dɑun] *the drain* [dreɪn].

4a. [d̪]—dentalized [d̪]; a heavy voiced fricative rather than a neat plosive [d].

"*I could* [kud̪] *dance, dance, dance* [d̪æns] *all night* [naɪt̪]."

4b. [ʔ]—glottalized [d]; as with a glottalized [t], but a heavier gutteral sound with the voiced [d].

*The settin'* [sɛʔɪn] *sun reddened* [rɛʔnʔ] *the whole mountain* [mɑʊnʔɪn] *top and the clouds* [klɑʊʔz] *above it.*

5. [k]—*kick* [kɪk]; the breath is stopped at the soft palate by the back of the tongue raised against the velum; released suddenly with a click.

*Make* [mek] *my hair curly* [kɝlɪ] *not kinky* [kɪŋkɪ].

5. [ʔ]—glottalized [k]; breath stopped at the glottis; released with a gutteral click.

*He's a lucky* [lʌʔɪ] *jockey* [dʒɒʔɪ] *to take* [teʔ] *that race.*

6. [g]—*gown* [gɑʊn]; the voiced twin of [k]; a harder sound with the voice added.

*Each girl* [gɝl] *wore a gown* [gɑʊn] *of golden* [goldn] *yellow.*

6. [ʔ]—glottalized [g]; as the glottalized [k], but a heavier sound with voice added.

*He staggered* [stæʔɝd] *over to the wagon* [wæʔn], *patted the wheel and began to sing:* "*Keep on rolling, wagon* [wæʔn] *wheels.*"

7. [m]—*ham* [hæm]; a warm hum floating through the nose and closed lips.

"*The Mombo* [mɒmboʊ] *is no dance for this Mambo* [mæmboʊ]," *she muttered* [mʌtɝd].

7. [m̃]—nasalized; a sharp, high-pitched hum floating through the nasal passage only; nasalized vowels with it, also.

"*Keeping time, time, time* [tãɪm̃] *in a sort of Runic rhyme* [rãɪm̃]."

8. [n]—*nine* [naɪn]; tip of the tongue on gum ridge; lips slightly open; gentle hum.

*From morning* [mɔ˞nɪŋ] *to noon* [nun] *to night* [naɪt] *Nina's* [ninəz] *heart danced* [danst] *the hours away.*

8. [ñ]—nasalized; sharp, high-pitched hum floating through the nasal passage only; pulls vowels into nose, also.

*This is a fine* [fãɪñ] *brand* [bræ̃ñd] *of Napa* [ñæ̃pə] *wine* [wãɪñ].

9a. [ŋ]—*hang* [hæŋ], *ink* [ɪŋk]; back of tongue humped against the soft palate; nasal hum.

*The child hurried along* [əlɒŋ], *skipping* [skɪpɪŋ] *rope and singing* [sɪŋɪŋ] *her songs* [sɒŋz].

9a. Substitutions for [ŋ]:
—[n]; an illiteracy; an error of mispronunciation made into a habit.

*Sampson's strength* [strɛnθ] *lay in the length* [lɛnθ] *of his hair.*

9b. [ŋg]—*single* (sɪŋgl]; in the mid-
~~... [ŋ] ( Ex-~~
cept verbal nouns or adjectives; as hanging [hæŋɪŋ] and hanger [hæŋə˞]).

*He lingered* [lɪŋgə˞d] *before the single* [sɪŋgl] *painting* [pentɪŋ] *hanging* [hæŋɪŋ] *in the room.*

9b. [ŋg]—[ŋ] followed always by the hard [g] at the ends of
~~words, ... dialect where~~
there has been Yiddish influence.

*Laughing* [lafɪŋ] *at her long* [lɒŋg] *face, he took her coat and hung* [hʌŋg] *it on a hanger* [hæŋgə˞].

10. [l]—*land* [lænd] ~~... "[b]ll.~~ liquid, voiced sound rolling off the sides of the tongue; initial [l] a light, clear [l]; final [l], a dark [l].

*Let* [lɛt] *the bells* [bɛlz] *toll* [tol] *loudly* [laʊdlɪ].

10a. [l]—inverted; tip of tongue ~~turned up ... covered.~~ inflexible, mouthed articulation.

*"Lula, lula, lula* [ļu:ļə] *lullaby* [ļʌļəbaɪ]."

10b. Substitutions for [l]; infantilisms to be corrected early:
—[w]—"*Flow* [fwoʊ] *gently* [dʒɛntwɪ], *Sweet Afton.*"

—[j]—(y)—*Nanna looks* [jʊks] *in the looking* [jʊkɪŋ] *glass* [gjæs].

10c. Adding vowels before final [l]; a drawled sound; affected. —[ə]—*You can't pull* [puəl] *the wool* [wuəl] *over my eyes.*

—[u]—*When I'm cold* [kould], *I roll* [roul] *up into a tight ball* [boul], *covers and all* [ɔul].

NOTE. Make Assignment XIII, Consonants You Habitually Mispronounce, a continuing assignment; begin it here. (pp. 91, Part II, the *Work Book*.) Make the greatest use of Assignments V, VII, IX and XIII, pp. 79, 81, 84 and 91, for your own progress.

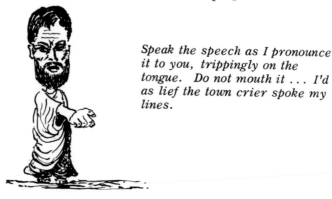

*Speak the speech as I pronounce it to you, trippingly on the tongue. Do not mouth it . . . I'd as lief the town crier spoke my lines.*

### THE ART OF ARTICULATION

James Thurber wrote in *The New Yorker;* October 25, 1960, that something bothers him, and that is "the pronunciation of words— crippled or wingless words that escape, all distorted, the careless human lips of our jittery time . . . ." But he hopes we can "restore the art of articulation, the dignity of diction, and thus improve the process of communication, for precision of communication is important, more important than ever, in our era of hair-trigger balances, when a false, or misunderstood, word may create as much disaster as a sudden thoughtless act . . . .

"A living language is an expanding language, to be sure, but care should take itself that the language does not crack like a dry stick in the process, leaving us all miserably muddling in a monstrous miasma of mindless and meaningless mumbling."

—JAMES THURBER in *The New Yorker*

# Chapter XIII

# The Fricatives And Semi-Vowels

| L A B I A L | | DENTAL | A V E O L A R | | | PALATAL | GLOTTAL |
|---|---|---|---|---|---|---|---|
| Bi-Labial | Labio-Dental | Tip to Teeth | Tip near Ridge | Blade near Ridge | Blade near Palate | | |
| Unv. ¦ V. | Unv. ¦ V. | Unv. ¦ V. | Unv. ¦ V. | Unv. ¦ V. | Unv. ¦ V. | Unv. ¦ V. | |
| [ʍ] ¦ [w]° | [f] ¦ [v] | [θ] ¦ [ð] | [s] ¦ [z] ¦ [r]° | [ʃ] ¦ [ʒ] | [j]° [h] | | |

Figure 30

The fricatives are by far the largest classification of consonants and are so-called because of the audible friction of the breath as it escapes through the very narrow, restricted passageways made by the articulators for these consonants, voiced and unvoiced. Again it is important to exercise control over the amount and force of the breath when enunciating the fricative consonants to avoid heavy over-aspiration, such as noisy, long [s] and [ʃ], long, windy [ ] ... [f] and [v].

**BI-LABIAL FRICATIVES:** [ʍ] as in WHERE, WHAT, WHISTLE
[w] as in WEAR, WATT, WIND

| IPA | DMS | |
|---|---|---|
| 1. [ʍ] | (wh) | Unvoiced |
| 2. [w] | (w) | Voiced |

S P E L L I N G S
1. *wh*istle, c*h*oir, q*u*iet.
2. *w*ind, *wh*y (an exclamation)

The word *whistle* is a good key word for the voiceless sound of [ʍ]; the puckering of the lips for a whistle is the correct lip shape for both [ʍ] and [w]. The tip of the tongue is placed against the lower front teeth while the blade of the tongue stretches up toward the palate. This is almost the same position of the tongue for the vowel [u], and the

---

*Also called semi-vowels.

pursed shape of the lips is the same. It is not surprising, then, that the voiced [w] is also called a semi-vowel. Too often in this country the voiced [w] is substituted for its unvoiced twin [ʍ].* This should be avoided, for confusion of meaning can often occur with such a substitution. There is a surprising number of words with completely different meanings which would sound exactly alike if the initial *wh* (unvoiced) were pronounced as the voiced [w]. Consider these words, to mention only a few:

> where—wear
> what—watt
> when—wenn
> while—wile
> which—witch
> why—wye

Now read this sentence from a well-known poem: "*The wind's like a whetted knife.*" There is considerable difference between a *whetted* [ʍɛtɪd] and a *wetted* [wɛtɪd] knife.

*THE LABIO-DENTAL FRICATIVE:* [f] as in FINE, LIFE, SOFTEN
[v] as in VERY, DRIVE, LIVID

IPA   DMS
1. [f]   (f) Unvoiced
2. [v]   (v) Voived

S P E L L I N G S
1. *fife*, mu*ff*in, tele*ph*one, lau*gh*.
2. *v*erge, fli*vv*er, o*f*, Ste*ph*en.

This pair of fricatives is one of two pairs of consonants that involve the teeth.† The [f] and [v] are made by bringing the lower lip up to meet the upper teeth, then sending breath or voiced breath through the spaces between the upper and lower teeth as through the sluice gate of a dam. As with all consonants, these should be neatly articulated, not dropped out of existence, as is sometimes the case when they come into conjunction with other consonants; for example, *fifth* [fɪfθ] not [fɪθ].

---

*Some phoneticians believe this unvoiced [ʍ] is gradually disappearing from American speech. This author does not share that opinion.

†All too frequently the [t] and [d] are *incorrectly* made with the tongue against the teeth, producing a noisy fricative instead of a clean plosive [t] and [d].

## THE DENTAL FRICATIVES: [θ] as in THIN, FOURTH, ETHICS
### [ð] as in THEN, WITH, WEATHER

*IPA*  *DMS*

1. [θ]  (th) Unvoiced
2. [ð]  (th) Voiced

S P E L L I N G S

1. *th*ink.
2. *th*ere, ba*the*.

To make this pair of consonants move the tip of the tongue forward to touch the edge of both upper and lower front teeth. (The tip may protrude between the teeth very slightly.) Now, send breath or voice forward through this imperfect dam of the tongue and teeth.

With those whose first language is English there is little difficulty with these dental consonants, [θ] and [ð]. The tip of the tongue flies to the edge of the teeth with the greatest of ease, as a rule, though some may find it difficult to make [θ] and [ð] in certain consonant combinations. In rapid or careless speech the voiced [ð] tends to disappear in combinations found in such words as *widths*, often pronounced [wɪdz] instead of [wɪðz], or *clothes*, as [kloz] instead of [kloðz].

With those whose first language~~~~~~~~~~~~~~~~~~~~~~~~~ German or French, however, the pronunciation of the English *th* will probably be [t] or [d], which is the sound of *th* in German and French.

## TIP-OF-TONGUE—ALVEOLAR FRICATIVES:
### [s] as in SO, BOSS, MISTER
### [z] as in ZOO, BUZZ, DESIRE

*IPA*  *DMS*

1. [s]  (s) Unvoiced
2. [z]  (z) Voiced

S P E L L I N G S

1. *s*ee, *s*auce, *s*cene, lo*ss*, *s*chism.
2. *z*ero, fu*zz*, bee*s*, di*s*cern, de*ss*ert, *X*erxe*s*.

To make this pair of consonants, the tip of the tongue is high in the front of the mouth, near the upper gum ridge, but *it touches nothing*. The sibilant hissing sound that results when unvoiced breath is emitted through the small space *between the tip of the tongue and the gum ridge* should be of a fine sharpness and very short in length. This is the [s] consonant, the most often used and the noisiest of all English consonants. These two facts account for its being the most noticeable and obtrusive when it is wrongly articulated. As an initial consonant, it must not be anticipated and hissed at length before the vowel is sounded. The following *vowel* may be long or short, but the initial *s* is always very short. Touch the [s] very lightly and follow immediately with the vowels in this sentence and the two will seem almost to be one sound: *See* [si:] *the sailor* [seɪlɚ] *sitting* [sɪtɪŋ] *on the sail* [seɪl].

The [z], as we have said, is made in the same way, with the tip of the tongue high and near the gum ridge, but not touching it. The difference between [s] and [z], of course, is simply that the [z] has voice. Un-voicing the final [z] is another instance of foreign influence in some speech patterns. It is very confusing to foreigners learning English that the letter *s* of English plural nouns and third person singular verbs is often pronounced [z]; e.g., heads [hɛdz], sees [si:z], leaves [li:vz].*

Unfortunately, with such a prominently sharp sound, there are many ways in which it may be mispronounced resulting in a thickened [ʃ], or a long, noisy, strong [s], or even whistling sounds for the [s]. Most of these errors are called lisps. In addition to the obvious substitution of [θ] for [s] there are numerous other forms of lisps, or thickening of the sharp edge of the [s]. The *dorsal* lisp is the most common and is made by keeping the tongue against the lower front teeth. It is possible to make a fairly good [s] in this position if the next sound is a vowel, but if [s] is followed by a consonant, as in *stop*, the tongue in the dorsal position is too inflexible to make the second consonant neatly.

To make [s] lightly and clearly as a fine, short, sharp sibilant, and [z] with a good clear voiced "buzz," great flexibility of the tongue is required, and of the tip of the tongue in particular. Once more you are admonished to develop this flexibility by intelligent and faithful practice. Turn to Exercise XIV, p. 198, Part II, the *Work Book*. Read the directions and notes carefully and repeat the phrases over and over.

### TIP OF TONGUE—ALVEOLAR FRICATIVE:
[r] as in ROSE, SPRING

*IPA    DMS*
[r]    (r) Voiced

S P E L L I N G S
red, *r*hyme, car*r*ot

This voiced consonant is made by sending voice through a narrow passage-way between the blade of the tongue raised nearly to the hard palate and a still smaller passageway between the tip of the tongue and the gum ridge. A vowel-like resonance chamber is made within the mouth, and the voiced [r] takes on somewhat the character of a vowel. It may, therefore, be called a semi-vowel along with the voiced [w] and [j], especially when

---

*See Chap. 11 p. 101. Observations on Spelling and Pronouncing Consonants.

we consider the quick tongue action smoothly gliding into the following vowel position.

Notice that there is a lift of the tongue in making this sound, *not* a turning back of the tip of the tongue. Following a vowel a turn-back action creates a pocket to catch the sound and invert it. The inverted [ɻ]*, too often heard in the middle west, has a particuarly bad effect on the preceding vowels, tending to cover them and generally cause them to lose their distinctive character.† As has been noted elsewhere, the [r] takes on great variability in American speech. In the East and South there is no final [r]; *car* is [kɑ:];*mark* [mɑ:k] rhyming with *mock; bother* ends in the weak vowel [ə]. Where a word ending in *r* precedes one beginning with a vowel the *r* tends to initiate the following words; for example: *The car is parked* [kɑrɪz pɑ˞:kt]; and *mother-in-law* [mʌðərɪnlɔ].‡ Because of the danger of inversion of the [r] with its accompanying tension at the back of the mouth, decidedly tight and unpleasant tonal quality and vowel distortion, a great many educated and cultured people prefer to follow the Eastern pattern of dropping the [r] from their speech. Good General ____ ____ ____ however, which stems from the educated pattern of the Middle West and West, sounds the [ɹ] ____ where it appears in words.

### BLADE OF TONGUE—ALVEOLAR FRICATIVES:
[ʃ] as in SURE, WISH, SPECIAL
[ʒ] as in AZURE, MEASURE

IPA     DMS
1. [ʃ]   (sh) Unvoiced
2. [ʒ]   ____ ____

SPELLINGS
1. sure, hu*sh*, fi*ss*ion, man-sion, no*ti*on, cons*ci*ence, o*ce*an, ma*ch*ine, pre*ci*ous.
2. a*z*ure, mea*s*ure, vi*si*on, gara*g*e, bra*z*ier.

This pair of consonants is closely related to [s] and [z], but much thicker in effect because the space between the blade (not the tip) ____ ____ and the gum ridge is larger than the tiny aperture that accounts for the [s] when the *tip* of the tongue is brought up close to the gum ridge. Again the difference between the [ʃ] and its voiced twin [ʒ] is the fact of vibration of the vocal bands for [ʒ]. Both [ʃ] and [ʒ] frequently fol-

---

*Written phonetically as [ɻ], with [.] below the [r].
†For further observations of the influence of [r] on preceding vowels see chapters 8, 9, 10 discussing specific vowels: [ɪ], [ɛ], [ɜ], [ɑ:], [ɔ:], [ʊ].
‡Curiously enough you may hear many people from Massachusetts add [r] at the end of a word when it should not be there; for example: *That is the law* [lɔ:r]. *The very idea* [aɪdi:r]!

low closely on [t] and [d] respectively. The letters *ch* are usually pronounced [tʃ]; e.g., *church* [tʃɜtʃ], *chop* [tʃɒp]. As we have noted, the so-called "soft g," as in *ginger*, is really two voiced sounds, [dʒ]; so, too, the English *j*, as in *judge*. Thus *ginger* phonetically is [dʒɪndʒɚ] and *judge* is [dʒʌdʒ].

### PALATAL FRICATIVE: [j] as in YELL, HALLELUJAH, ONION

IPA     DMS

[j]    (y)  Voiced

S P E L L I N G S

*y*et, hallelu*j*ah, lor*g*nette, un*i*on.

To make this consonant, let the middle of the tongue hump up near the hard palate, then send voice through the mouth over the hump of the tongue. The resulting sound is almost like the vowel [ɪ] and is often called a semi-vowel; it is the sound of the initial consonant in *yes, yet, yellow.* An initial *y* beginning a word is pronounced as the semi-vowel [j], but a final *y* is always pronounced as the vowel [ɪ]. Another interesting observation about this semi-vowel consonant is that in some words it is pronounced where no written consonant is to be seen. It is inserted between an initial consonant and a following [u] vowel, *when* that sound is spelled with *u* or *ew* (except after *l, r,* and sometimes *t*). This is not the case if the [u] sound is spelled with *oo*. Note these words spelled with *oo* and *u* or *ew* in the following phrases:

> *The noon news.* [ðə nu:n nju:z]
>
> *Do pay dues now* [du: peɪ dju:z nɑu].
>
> *True blue* [tru: blu:]

### GLOTTAL FRICATIVE: [h] as in HIM

IPA     DMS

[h]    (h)  Unvoiced

S P E L L I N G S

*h*it, w*h*o.

The vocal bands are drawn toward each other enough to permit breath to cause friction as it passes between them, but not close enough to generate voice. Nothing within the mouth is involved in making this consonant, so the tongue and the lips can shape the oral chamber into the correct resonance chamber for the following vowel. Thus the consonant and the vowel may be sounded almost simultaneously, the glottal, unvoiced aspirate quickly followed by the vocalized vowel stream. Care should be taken not to overdo this glottal consonant to avoid covering the following vowel with too much breath and robbing it of clarity.

At this point finish Assignment XII for the Fricative Consonants. (pp. 89-90, Part II,. the *Work Book*.)

## TO SUMMARIZE

The twenty-three English consonants should neatly bracket the twenty-five vowels and diphthongs of our language into the syllables of our English words. To pronounce these syllables and assimilate them fluently into words and the words into sentences requires training of the articulators. The golden mean between the all too common "Murrcan" speech of Mr. and Mrs. Joe Elision* and the pedanticism of the over carefully enunciated speech of a perfectionist is something for every person to find for himself. To arrive at this golden mean of easy, natural speech, which is also clear-cut and beautiful, you must train yourself first by sharp listening and obse........,              .......h-sized in Part I. and then by careful practice in the formation of the vowels and consonants of the language.

We would remind you again that careful techniques of breath control are as important for good articulation as for fundamental voice production. The force of the breath for ordinary speaking should be very slight, and there must be no interference with its easy movement through the glottis—no glottal stop before syllables beginning with a vowel. We ... .. ... ... the unvoiced breath only very slightly on unvoiced consonants, a trifle more of the voiced bi.... .. ...... consonants, but in the vowels the breath should be completely transmuted into clear tone.

Remember that the consonants give definition to speech and that laxity and slovenliness in making them result in unclear speech, difficult to understand. Therefore, to make yourself easily understood work to gain flexibility of the articulators, in order that by their neat, clean action in enunciation you add sense to the sound of your voice. Then to articulation is added significance of meaning by the changes within the voice itself—pitch and tone, variance of loudness, and many other variations—to express subtleties, shades and nuances of meaning.

---

*Chapter 11.

# PRONUNCIATIONS
## THE FRICATIVES AND SEMI-VOWELS

NOTE. As in Chapter 12, read aloud the sentences below in both columns. Sound the IPA symbols as written and listen with concentration to each consonant you make, correct and incorrect. Give all vowels careful attention, also, for their correct sounding.

### DESIRABLE

1. [ʍ]—*white* [ʍaɪt]; blowing unvoiced air through the pursed lips; always spelled *wh;* always an initial consonant.

    *When* [ʍɛn] *the whistle* [ʍɪsl] *blows, boys, begin whittling* [ʍɪtlɪŋ].

2. [w]—*wide* [waɪd]—almost an [u] vowel blown through the pursed lips: often called a semi-vowel.

    *What a wonderous* [wʌndrəs] *place is the wide, wide* [waɪd] *world* [wɝld].

3. [f]—*free* [fri:]; voiceless breath through the dam of the upper teeth on the lower lips.

    *Fred* [frɛd] *walked full* [fʊl] *five* [faɪv] *and a half* [haf] *miles before* [bɪfɚ]† *he got there.*

4. [v]—*very* [vɛrɪ], *even* [i:vn]; voiced twin of [f].

    *Vivian* [vɪvɪən] *avidly* [ævɪdlɪ] *avowed* [əvaʊd] *her faith in Verna* [vɝnə].

5. [θ]—*thimble* [θɪmbl], *e t h e r* [iθɚ]; tip of tongue against edge of upper and lower teeth; voiceless breath passing through the slightly parted teeth.

### UNDESIRABLE

1. Substitutions for [ʍ]:
   —[w]—voiced sound; s e m i-vowel; often changes the meaning of words.

    *Where* [wɛ] *the wind's whistle* [wɪsl] *is sharp as a whetted* [wɛtɪd] *knife.*

2. Substitutions for [w]:
   —[v] foreign influence from the German.

    *Why* [vaɪ] *will* [vɪl] *you do that* [dæt].*

3. [fʰ]—overaspirated; too long and too strong a force of breath before the following vowel is sounded.

    *Fight, fight, fight* [fʰaɪt] *for* [fʰɔ] *freedom* [fʰri:dəm].

4. Substitutions for [v]:
   —[w]; foreign influence from the German.

    *Verna* [wɝnə] *was* [vas] *very* [wɛrɪ] *grateful for Vivian's* [wɪwɪənz] *faith in her.*

5. Substitutions for [θ]:
   —[t] foreign influence from German.

    *Think* [tɪŋk] *it over and you'll thank* [tæŋk] *me for it.*

---

*Substituting [d] for *th* [ð] is also a foreignism from the German.
†General American (GA).

*Think* [θɪŋk] *of the ethics* [εθɪks] *of things* [θɪŋz].

—[s] foreign influence from the French.

*"Thank* [sæŋk] *you," she hissed through* [srʊ:] *her thin* [sm] *lips.*

6. [ð]—*then* [ðεn], *rather* [raðɚ]; the voiced twin of [θ] above.

*Then* [ðεn] *and there* [ðε] *they* [ðeɪ] *voted for the* [ðə] *plan.*

6. Substitutions for [ð]:
—[d]; foreign influence from German:*

*The* [də] *bride's m o t h e r* [mʌdɚ] *and father* [fɑdɚ] *were there* [dεr] *also.*

—[z]—foreign influence from French:

*Then* [zεn] *they* [ze] *went over to the* [zi] *other* [ʌzɚ] *side.*

7. [s]—*sense* [sεns]; unvoiced; sent ̲ ̲ ̲ ̲ ̲ ̲ ̲ ̲ ̲ aperture be-tween the tip of the tongue and the upper gum ridge; a fine, sharp, short hiss.

*Jane Austin* [ɔ:stɪn] *wrote "Sense* [sεns] *and Sensibility"* [sεnsɪbɪlɪtɪ].

7a. LISPS: varying degrees of thick-ness of the [s]; deviations from ̲ ̲ ̲ fine sharpness of a good [s]; tip of the tongue touches the teeth or gum ridges.

7b. Substitutions for [s]:
—[θ]—the tongue between the teeth; an infantilism.

*Since* [θɪnθ] *you say* [θe] *so ̲ ̲ ̲ it must* [mʌθ] *be so* [θoʊ].

8. [z]—*zero* [zɪroʊ], *raise* [reɪz]; the voiced twin of [s]; a thick buzz.

*She rose* [roʊz] *to make two o b s e r v ations* [ɒbzɝveʃʌnz] *about planting azaleas* [əzeɪlɪəz] *and roses* [roʊzɪz].

8. Substitutions for [z];
—[s]—unvoiced sibilant, espec-ially for the final [z] sound; for-eignism.

*Because* [bɪkɔ:s] *you told me things* [θɪŋs] *would be better, I ordered these* [ði:s].

9. [r]—*ran* [ræn]; voiced breath sent through small aperture be-tween blade of tongue near hard palate, tip of tongue near gum ridge.

9. [ɻ]—*error* [εɻəɻ]—a heavy *"er"* sound for a final [r]; tip of tongue turned up and back, in-verted, makes a pocket to catch the voice.

*See #2, Rt. column, p. 124.

"Ring [rɪŋ] *around* [ərɑʊnd] *the rosie* [roʊzɪ]," *sang the children* [-drɪn].

*They grew worse* [wɝs] *and worse* [wɝs] *before* [bɪfɔr] *they were* [wɝ] *forced* [fɔːr̥st] *to change their* [ðɛr] *ways.*

9b. Substitutions for [r]:
—[w]—for an initial [r]; an infantilism.

*Roll* [woʊl] *over, R o v e r* [woʊvɝ].

—[l]—for initial [r]; an infantilism.

*Right* [laɪt] *and wrong* [lɒŋ].

10. [ʃ]—*she* [ʃiː], *wish* [wɪʃ]; a broader sound than the fine [s]; blade of tongue raised toward the gum ridge.

*She* [ʃiː] *shrieked* [ʃrikt] *from shock* [ʃɒk] *a n d shivered* [ʃɪvɚd] *with fear.*

11. [ʒ]—*azure* [æʒʊɚ]; voiced twin of [ʃ].

*The large* [lɑrdʒ] *expanse of azure* [æʒʊɚ] *sky gave us immeasureable* [ɪmɛʒʊrəbl] *pleasure* [plɛʒʊɚ].

12. [j]—*yet* [jɛt]; the third semivowel; almost like [ɪ]; middle of tongue is raised near the hard palate.

*The yellow* [jɛlo] *tulips* [tjulɪps] *were very beautiful* [bjutɪful] *yesterday* [jɛstɚdɪ].

12. Substitutions for [j]:
—[i]—between initial consonant and a following [u];

*The dew* [diuː] *is on the tulips* [tiulɪps].

13. [h] — *h i m* [hɪm]; unvoiced breath through the narrowed glottis.

*He* [hi] *hummed* [hʌmd] *in harmony* [hɑrmənɪ] *to her* [hɝ] *singing.*

13. [hʰ]; overaspiration; too long and strong a force of breath before the vowel is sounded.

*The hollow* [hʰɒlo] *sound came from the hollow* [hʰɒloʊ] *log.*

# Index

**127**